MW01620481

THIRD EDITION

SHOWIT

Visit our website at showit.co.

Copywriting: Cassandra Campbell, Jihae Watson, Shamesha Sheffield, Karen Jezek, Elisa Watson, Jennifer Olmstead, Jeff Shipley, Elizabeth McCravy, Jessica Gingrich, Bernel Westbrook

Cover photo: Ryan Greenleaf

Design: Chris Misterek, Jed Smith, Nate Sees

ISBN 978-0-578-65947-3

Printed in China

Even the most out-of-the-box thinkers can, at times, find themselves in a creative rut. We've all been there. Maybe you're there right now. If you are, we see you, and we feel your frustration. What we've discovered is that we are rarely able to get out of those ruts on our own. When we get stuck in a rut, what we need is a fellow traveler to come alongside us, to take us by the hand, to offer some words of encouragement and then point us again in the right direction.

Consider this book a gift from your fellow travelers. In these pages you will find beauty and inspiration, and here and there you may come across something that speaks encouragement to you, something that points you in the right direction.

We all need others to help us along in our journeys. Creativity never flourishes in a vacuum. We need the stimulating presence and ideas of other creative minds to help motivate and sustain us in our own journeys. We have filled the pages of this book with websites created by 50 of those kinds of people. They have no doubt received creative motivation from others along the way, and we are delighted to share their work with you now, in hopes that it will provide creative motivation for you, too.

There's no need to walk your journey alone. This little book is simply one way to be reminded that you are in good company, and that the way ahead is beautiful.

Traveling with you,

TABLE OF CONTENTS

BRIAR'S ATLAS

BRIARSATLAS.COM

Any creative can relate to Oli Sansom's desire to "visibly stand out in an ever more crowded market of brilliant and intimidating talent." Instead of giving up or giving in, the photographer, and all around genius creative, took every opportunity to stand out using his online storefront. He proclaims that his ideal client is a "happy, layered" kind of person, and that is exactly what his website is. At every scroll BriarsAtlas.com chooses to go against the grain of anything you have ever seen. Oli chooses layered, visual movement and loads of cheeky copywriting to sway visitors into becoming clients. Brides and grooms will not only be booking, but passing the popcorn around as they show friends and family BriarsAtlas.com.

DESIGNED FROM SCRATCH

IN SHOWIT

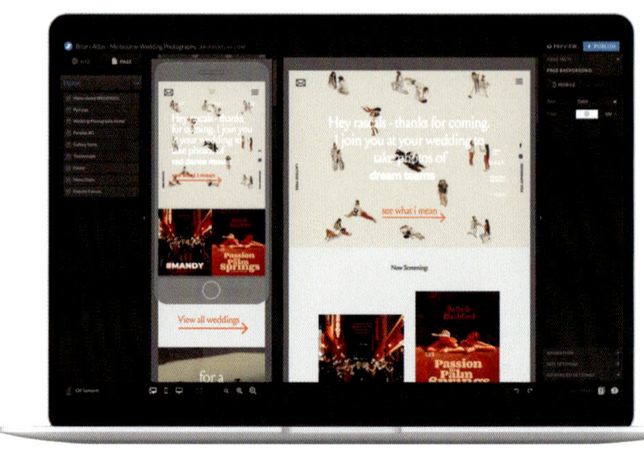

COLORS

#111111

#3C3C3C

#606060

#EE5946

#B1BFC9

#E7E5E2

#FAF8F5

#FFFFFF

TYPEFACES

LOUIZE REGULAR

Oswald Normal

Montserrat

Now Screening:

Melbourne Town Hall becomes Matt and Andy Town Hall (for but an hour or more)

Ballis & Blachford

Passion in Palm Springs

Keith Urban didn't actually turn up, and it turns out he wasn't actually needed

View all weddings

for a good time and a long time

CHEERS BABE PHOTO

CHEERSBABEPHOTO.COM

Their photos are "bright & poppy and full of joy" so it only makes sense that their website is too! With Jess behind the camera, her husband Chris (the design wizard) stepped in behind the computer to bring her images to life. CheersBabePhoto.com is stocked with catchy copy, super-fun parallax, and graphics that will make you feel as happy as that time you first tried your favorite fruity candy. Sherbet colors and joy-filled couples provide the background to Cheers Babe Photo's real message: "We want people to visit our site and feel happy, inspired and super excited to get married." With that refreshing approach to the first day of marriage, brides-to-be are going to want to lock down their dates immediately.

DESIGNED FROM SCRATCH

IN SHOWIT

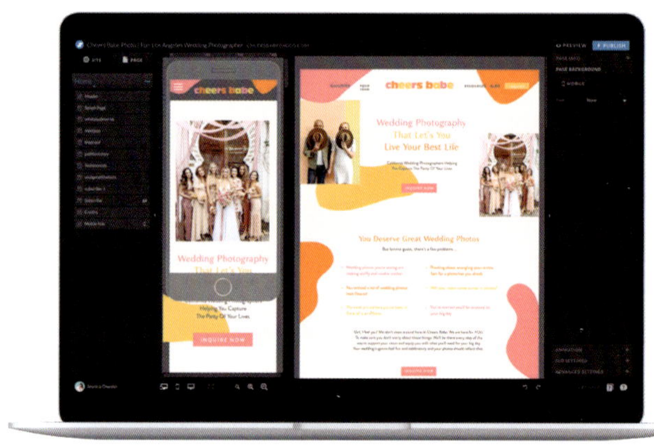

COLORS

#FE899B

#FF840C

#FEC232

#FFCCCC

#FFE6CE

#707070

#FFFFFF

#FFF2EB

TYPEFACES

Granville Light

Brandon Regular

Brandon Bold

GALLERIES YOUR TEAM **cheers babe** RESOURCES BLOG INQUIRE

Wedding Photography That Let's You Live Your Best Life

California Wedding Photographers Helping You Capture The Party Of Your Lives

INQUIRE NOW

cheers babe

Wedding Photography That Let's You Live Your Best Life

California Wedding Photographers Helping You Capture The Party Of Your Lives

You Deserve Great Wedding Photos

But lemme guess, there's a few problems ...

- Wedding photos you're seeing are looking stuffy and cookie-cutter.
- Thinking about wrangling your entire fam for a photo has you shook
- You noticed a lot of wedding photos look filtered
- Will your vision come across in photos?
- The most pro camera you've been in front of is an iPhone.
- You're worried you'll be stressed on your big day

Girl, I feel you! We don't mess around here at Cheers Babe. We are here for YOU. To make sure you don't worry about these things. We'll be there every step of the way to support your vision and equip you with what you'll need for your big day. Your wedding is gonna feel fun and celebratory and your photos should reflect that.

INQUIRE NOW

BTW, Who Are We?

We are an LA based wedding photography team, led by our founder, Jess. That's me in the pic - heyyy! Our photos are bright & poppy and full of joy, capturing the most celebratory and emotional moments of the biggest day of your life.

Beyond snapping your most cherished memories, we'll help you relax, laugh, and feel confident in front of the camera — never awkward. We build sincere friendships with our couples to create the kind of trust and bond that makes for gorgeous photos.

MEET THE TEAM

Let's Talk Style

"Fashions fade, style is eternal."
-Yves Saint Laurent

You want your wedding photos to be colorful, fun and real. Not light and airy or dark and moody. Our style is true to color (especially when it comes to spot-on skin tones) because that filtered editing trend will fade and your bright & crisp wedding photos will look timeless.

We'll direct you with natural movement (and definitely some dance moves) to achieve a casual & chill look in your photos instead of putting you in awkward poses that you'll feel totally uncomfortable in. We don't like to brag, but we think we're pretty fun to be around - Jess is always cracking jokes to make the bridal party laugh while trying her best to remember everyone's name. We also care a ton about making the process efficient and stress-free, which we achieve through scouting locations ahead of time and lots of prep work with your vendors.

Lastly, we pay special attention for those once-in-a-lifetime moments -- ya know, like the moment your mom zips up your dress or when your grandma wipes a tear from her eye during your vows. This is the real stuff -- the good stuff that you'll get to cherish forever. With us on your team, you'll feel like your best self on your wedding day and your photos will prove it!
Who's ready to party with us?

LOOK AT GALLERIES

How To Lock It Down

LOLA ROSE PHOTOGRAPHY

LOLAROSEPHOTOGRAPHY.COM

If there was any question as to whom Kelly's ideal clients are, they will instantly find the answer at LolaRosePhotography.com. With the first click, they are treated to a gorgeous slideshow focusing on "free spirits & adventurous souls." A quick scroll will reveal more of what makes Kelly's relationship with her clients so special. Splashes of metallic copper mixed with pops of natural elements ensures she stands out to the "not afraid to step off the beaten track" bride she seeks to attract. Kelly, who designer her site from scratch in Showit, seems to have thought of everything. Even tucked away on its own special page, Kelly has added her wedding films, which are a treat in themselves. And truly, the whole site is a treat for the senses.

DESIGNED FROM SCRATCH

IN SHOWIT

COLORS

#000000

#838383

#97A17A

#F2D9CA

#F9A695

#DFDEDA

#ECEBE8

#FFFFFF

TYPEFACES

Montserrat

Fjalla One

Lato Light

Heart Soul

lola rose
PHOTOGRAPHY

hello lovely lets have an adventure

ABOUT GALLERY INFO lola rose PHOTOGRAPHY LEARN CONTACT BLOG

Your wedding is the start of one of the biggest adventures of your life. Being chosen to capture these moments is a huge honour, and one I never take for granted.

It's such a special gift to be given a front row seat to the most important day of your lives, so I make it my mission to capture your story in a beautiful, meaningful & honest way. Embarrassing dad dancing, flower girl sulking, jagér bomb shot drinking, and ugly crying included.

If you've been searching for something more than just photographs then you're in the right place, because I believe that telling a great wedding story goes far deeper than just clicking the shutter...it needs to be felt by the heart...

Wedding Films
THIS WAY FOR THE ACTION >>

THE MINT SWEATER

THEMINTSWEATER.COM

The Mint Sweater is a community of like-minded women who desire to live a full and purposeful life. Founder and CEO Marnie Jayne is the creative mastermind behind this growing movement. She publishes helpful resources on the Mint Sweater blog, offers exclusive apparel through their online boutique, and organizes local gatherings for the community. This girl-powered website boldly communicates their vision with strength, and also cozy, softness, via their strong block fonts, and pops of mint and cursive script. Basically, the Mint Sweater community is one that you are surely going to want to be a part of if you need support and encouragement for your big dreams. You are meant to be the leading lady of your life, and the Mint Sweater will not let you forget that.

DESIGNED FROM SCRATCH

IN SHOWIT

COLORS

TYPEFACES

TOKYO REGULAR

TOKYO OUTLINE

Quicksand Normal

Quicksand Light

Lato Italic

Fjalla One

PEACHY MERGED REGULAR

Marshmallow

Oswald Normal

Oswald Light

ABOUT BLOG SHOP CONTACT EVENTS COMMUNITY

the MINT SWEATER

A BLOG

A COMMUNITY

& CURATED SHOP

OH HEY GIRL,

we're not just a biz about sweaters.
we are the babes who help you feel effortlessly beautiful in your sweater, confident in who you are and where you are going, in love with the friendships you've built, & feel like you are ACTUALLY having fun in your life again.

let's get this party started!

she's a one girl

REVOLUTION

Like Arthur in The Holiday said, "In the movies, we have the leading lady and we have the best friend. You, are a leading lady, but for some reason you are behaving like the best friend. And as Iris responds, "You're so right. You're supposed to be the leading lady of your own life."

GIRL, IT'S TIME TO START BEING THE LEADING LADY OF YOUR OWN LIFE.

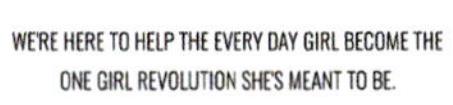

WE'RE HERE TO HELP THE EVERY DAY GIRL BECOME THE ONE GIRL REVOLUTION SHE'S MEANT TO BE.

Through our blog, community, and online boutique we provide the resources, tools, and style to equip and inspire every leading lady to build a fulfilling and purposeful life for herself.

READY TO MAKE CHANGE FINALLY HAPPEN FOR YOURSELF,
BUT NOT SURE WHERE TO START?
GET YOUR FREE SOUL SEARCHING STARTERS GUIDE

SNAG YOUR COPY NOW

THE BLOG

CAREER

BEAUTY & STYLE

CREATIVITY

WELLNESS

CULTURE

HOSTESS

FULFILLMENT

Here, women feel seen, heard, and valued. They have a place where they feel they belong. In our community, women walk away feeling fulfilled and loved.

FRIENDSHIPS

A place to make new friends and a community to help you cultivate genuine long-lasting friendships.

CONNECTIONS

In a community it's easy to make connections, but here at The Mint Sweater women feel connected with one another no matter how near or far they may be.

HEART-TO-HEARTS

Where stories are shared, vulnerability is welcomed and walls are broken down so women no longer feel alone. Those are the heart-to-heart moments shared in our community.

THE MINT SWEATER COMMUNITY

The Mint Sweater Community is a movement. Through our online community in our Facebook Group and hashtags #mintsweatergirl and

let us direct you!

ABOUT

BLOG

BOUTIQUE

E-BOOK

COMMUNITY

CONTACT

IN THE DETAILS DARLING

INTHEDETAILSDARLING.COM

Created as a cozy welcome spot for all those overwhelmed "sweet CEOs", IntheDetailsDarling.com has hit its mark. With a subtle feminine palette, the frazzled entrepreneur will instantly feel calmed and ready to receive Jenna's powerful message: "Freedom is not an impossible dream." The owner of this website has a secret weapon in knowing what you and your business needs. Partnering with Abigail Dyer Design, the other secret weapon in her business is her website. Through her uplifting copy, clean images, and videos of Jenna, you get a sense that her online home probably feels like her actual home: Comfortable, inviting, and safe. This brand manager has a deep desire to leave everything, and everyone, better than she found them.

DESIGNED BY

ABIGAIL DYER
ABIGAIL DYER DESIGN

ABIGAILDYERDESIGN.COM

COLORS

#333333
#58595B
#C7AFAF
#E5D1D1
#F2E7E7
#EDE5DD
#EFE4E4
#FFFFFF

TYPEFACES

Assistant Light
Assistant Semi Bold
Quincy Regular
Quincy Light Italic
Paris Regular

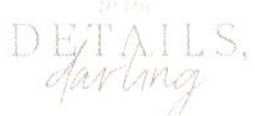

sweet ceo

listen up:

freedom is not an impossible dream.

you don't have to clone yourself for your business to grow.
you don't have to sacrifice your life, work crazy hours, or give up the thought of ever going on a vacation again.

book that flight, take a real weekend, watch your business thrive.

i'm jenna,

you can probably find me obsessing over my next adventure with my husband, with a french 75 in hand, i'm ready to uncover a process, streamline a system, implement the magic that can help take your business back to dream status faster than you can say... wait, did i just clone myself?

picture this

chief empowered officer (n.):

a business owner empowered by her ability to stay in her zone of genius, serve her clients + customers with crazy heart, and have a business that allows her to be completely present for the most important things in life.

let's trade that everything kind of exhaustion for the enjoyment and empowerment that comes with letting someone else in to not only manage what's there, but to make it even better.

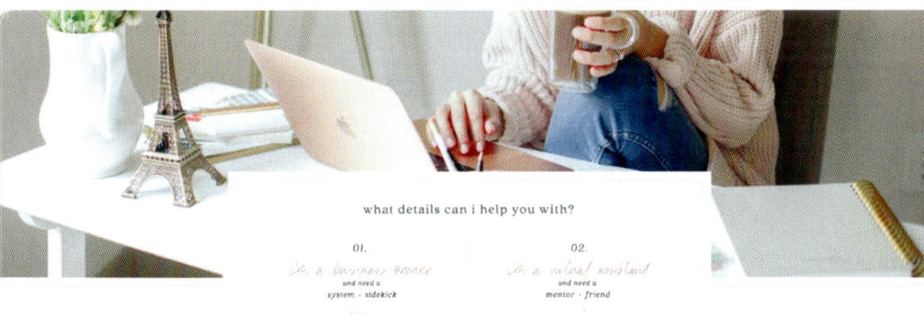

what details can i help you with?

01.

02.

love notes

"How can I ever express my gratitude for what Jenna has done and brought to my business? She is thoughtful, professional, efficient and a serious GODSEND. I owe Jenna a lot of what has made my business grow over 30% each year. You need a Jenna in Your Life."

heather christoper, heather christopher travel consulting

need balance in your business?

Email

First name

in the

DETAILS,

darling

sweet ceo

listen up:

freedom is not an impossible dream.

you don't have to clone yourself for your business to grow.
you don't have to sacrifice your life, work crazy hours, or give up the thought of ever going on a vacation again.

THE DARING ONES

THEDARINGONES.COM

The folks behind The Daring Ones Photography "love working with down to earth people who aren't afraid to go off the beaten path a bit." Darian and Amy are a husband and wife team that are experts at finding "perfection in your imperfections" in the most interesting places. With Alisabeth Designs, the couple has created a brand and website that perfectly reflects them and their ideal clients - fun and adventurous, but also warm and charming. Using dreamy earth tones, their vision for a bold brand on their site has finally come to life. Of their new website, they say "not only does it make us feel more confident about what we've created but it makes our couples more confident in our work!"

DESIGNED BY

SARAH ALISABETH
ALISABETH DESIGNS

ALISABETHDESIGNS.COM

TYPEFACES

Rylan

Cairo Grotesque Regular

Margo

ADVENTUROUS PHOTOS FOR ADVENTUROUS LOVERS

HOME
OUR STORY
INVESTMENT
PORTFOLIO
BLOG
SAY HEY

the daring ones
PHOTOGRAPHY

HOME OUR STORY INVESTMENT PORTFOLIO BLOG CONTACT

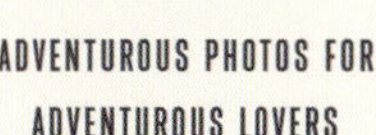

ADVENTUROUS PHOTOS FOR ADVENTUROUS LOVERS

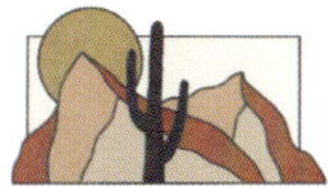

the daring ones
PHOTOGRAPHY

LOVING SOMEONE IS NEVER THE WRONG IT

MENU

here's the thing

Choosing love is seriously the greatest adventure any human can embark on.

IT'S NOT ALWAYS EASY BUT ITS ALWAYS WORTH IT!

We're here for the ones who are daring enough to take that leap of faith and say "I choose this human for the rest of my life". We're here to capture every moment of that journey, perfect and imperfect, honest, and true to who you guys are. We want you to remember how you felt. Every little moment, every big feeling, we want to capture it all!

About Us

Come on over and stalk us and then lets' go on a double date, take some rad photos, and have a freaking good time!

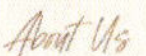

COME LEARN MORE ABOUT US

K OUT MORE

OUR RECENT ADVENTURES

PORTFOLIO

Black Sands Beach San

WORD ON THE STREET IS...

"These guys are the most incredible team of photographers I've ever met...."

These guys are the most incredible team of photographers I've ever met, and are worth their weight in gold. We hired this dynamic duo to shoot our wedding last September and the photos were beautifully shot and edited — they truly were able to capture the feeling and vibe of our special day. And, their photos were so awesome that they are now printed all over our house (thanks for making us embrace our narcissism, guys! lol). Not only is their work incredible, but they were so easy and fun to work with. Having a team of photographers definitely helped with being able to capture all the special moments pre-ceremony and was special to work with a couple at a wedding who embody love and reverence for one another.

- Victoria & Parker

LET US CAPTURE THE BEST OF YOUR LOVE

the daring

A bit of info

The Daring Ones is a husband and wife destination wedding photographer team based

Come explore with us

HOME OUR STORY INVESTMENT

HANNAH K. PHOTOGRAPHY

HANNAHKPHOTOGRAPHY.CO.UK

Hannah is a redheaded American girl who crossed the ocean to chase her dreams. She is now in England, growing her photography business, as well as mentoring other photographers. Her style is natural and bright which you can see immediately in her custom website built by Alisabeth Designs. Her site is very welcoming and makes you want to stay to see every glorious image. The colors and font choices have come together to create such a fun and organic vibe. And the site is so interactive, from her Bucket List, to the script font that makes it sound like she is talking directly to YOU. No matter whether you are in the US or England, going to hannahkphotography.co.uk is worth the trip!

DESIGNED BY

SARAH ALISABETH
ALISABETH DESIGNS

ALISABETHDESIGNS.COM

TYPEFACES

Raleway Normal

Bodoni

Roadtrip

Hey, friend! I am so, so glad you're here!!

MY NAME IS HANNAH AND I AM A DESTINATION WEDDING AND LIFESTYLE PHOTOGRAPHER BASED IN WARWICKSHIRE, ENGLAND!

I'm a redheaded American girl living in the UK and I am most passionate about photographing intimate and relaxed weddings for fun and joyful couples who are adventurous at heart.

Pull up a chair, grab a glass of sauvignon blanc and have a look around!

come read the
BLOG

are you here for...

PHOTOGRAPHY?

Whether you're craving photos with your love on your wedding day or images that capture your lifestyle, brand or obsession with adventure, I'm here to make your personality come to life!

WEDDINGS | LIFESTYLE

MENTORSHIP?

I am so passionate about helping others pursue their dream jobs of being full-time photographers. I love to inspire and encourage while also giving practical advice and hands-on experience.

MORE ABOUT MENTORING

"...It was the easiest decision I made in the whole of the wedding planning process..."

HELEN & JAMES ORCHARDLEIGH ESTATE, SOMERSET

"Hannah is such a wonderful person and a brilliant photographer. I approached her to take our wedding photos after a recommendation from a friend, and it was the easiest decision I made in the whole of the wedding planning process. She has such a personable approach to her photography, she really wants to get to know you and that comes through in beautifully natural photos."

@hannahkphotography

5 WAYS TO MAKE YOUR WEBSITE BETTER RIGHT NOW

with JEN OLMSTEAD *&* JEFF SHIPLEY
from TONIC SITE SHOP

1 *Review your website*

One of the most common problems we see online is pure website neglect: a small business owner launches a new website and then doesn't touch it (or look at it) again until the sudden urge to rebrand strikes three years later.

But like great businesses, great websites aren't just made: they evolve. They should grow, improve, and change over time to fit their owners, who are growing and changing, too.

So, if you haven't looked at your website lately, that's a great place to start. To begin, open your website and browse every page with fresh eyes. Try to look at your site from the perspective of your ideal client, and make changes to move them to reach out and connect with you.

2 *Update Your Galleries*

We allllll know you're sitting on batches of beautiful images from last season's work, but it's easy to feel overwhelmed by the task of culling them all, or like you should just wait until you have a new website you love to showcase work you love.

But while the perfect next website is always out there, even a mediocre website with a portfolio laser targeted to the kind of clients you want to work with is a HUGE improvement over what you have in the meantime. Curation goes a long way, friends! If you can add even 10 images that "show you what you want to shoot" (or sell, if you're not a photographer) to your site, it'll be worth the half hour spent doing so. One of those shots might be the one that clinches it for the prospective client shopping your site!

3 *Refresh your about section images.*

Alert: This is one of the easiest ways to make your website feel fresh and updated. Hire someone to shoot some updated headshots, consider in the process how you make them feel the most like your brand (clothing, location, styling), and pop those puppies up on social media and throughout your site. A new set of about images is like a mini-makeover – everything looks just a little more fresh, with minimal effort.

4 *Get yourself some social proof (and show it better)*

We harp on this a lot, but updating your website shouldn't only be a "you" undertaking. This is a GREAT time to ask for feedback from your friends, peers, and even past clients – "I'm working on my website" is a reason to reach out that everyone immediately understands.

But don't just ask for feedback on your site: one of the easiest ways to ask clients for reviews is to tell them you're updating your website. Send a quick personal email to a few of your favorite clients from the past year that says something like, "Hey there, ___; I'm going through the process of updating my site (whew!), and I'd looove to feature you. Would you be willing to send over answers to a couple of questions about working with me?" Then add a few specific prompts to get the kind of feedback you're looking for.

When you have their answers, grab a few of the best quotes to highlight, and add those to your site (preferably with an image attached... hey there, quick and easy portfolio update!). Reviews are the BEST social proof that working with you is a great choice, and that solves a huge pain point for your potential client (who's wondering if booking you is indeed the great choice).

5 *If necessary, consider big changes.*

So, we've shared a few ways to make your current site better, but what if after #1, you're like, "Jen and Jeff, is this a 'BURN IT DOWN' situation?" Your site isn't connecting with your ideal client, it doesn't show you at your best, and it doesn't set you apart in your field? Well, especially if you're a photographer, this is absolutely the time to consider a new site design: before you move into your prime shooting season, so you can book, accept referrals, shoot, and move through the rest of the year with confidence in your online presence.

If you're looking for a custom design, nooooow is the time to inquire with a designer, since most book up very early in the year. If you'd like something beautiful up and running ASAP, we've designed a few sites we don't think you'll want to burn down... If you're in the market, check out the templates from our site shop at the link below.

We hope you feel inspired to make a few small, but significant changes that will leave you feeling more confident in the website you're presenting online. Let us know if you have any questions!

LEARN MORE FROM JEN & JEFF AT
TONICSITESHOP.COM

THE CAREERIST

THE-CAREERIST.COM

Why would someone leave a 200k salary to start a new business? To help others. Natasha Baker is the owner and powerhouse behind The Careerist, a luxury boutique consulting agency. She is passionate about serving women to help them find freedom in their careers. She, as well as her website, exudes power, presence, and a sense of adventure. And this is what she wants for her website visitors. Natasha's site was inspired by the Tonic Site Shop template *Amaretto*, and it has been fully customized by the incredible designer Amanda, of Amanda Burg Design Studio. The quintessential modern career woman will feel right at home at the-careerist.com, and will find a community of like minded boss ladies to join.

CUSTOMIZED BY

AMANDA BURG
AMANDA BURG DESIGN STUDIO

AMANDABURGDESIGN.COM

COLORS

#1A3A33

#D9B1A3

#F9F9F8

#050505

#000000

#808080

#CACACA

#FFFFFF

TYPEFACES

Cormorant Normal

Cormorant Medium

Cormorant Bold

Cormorant Italic

Nimbus Bold

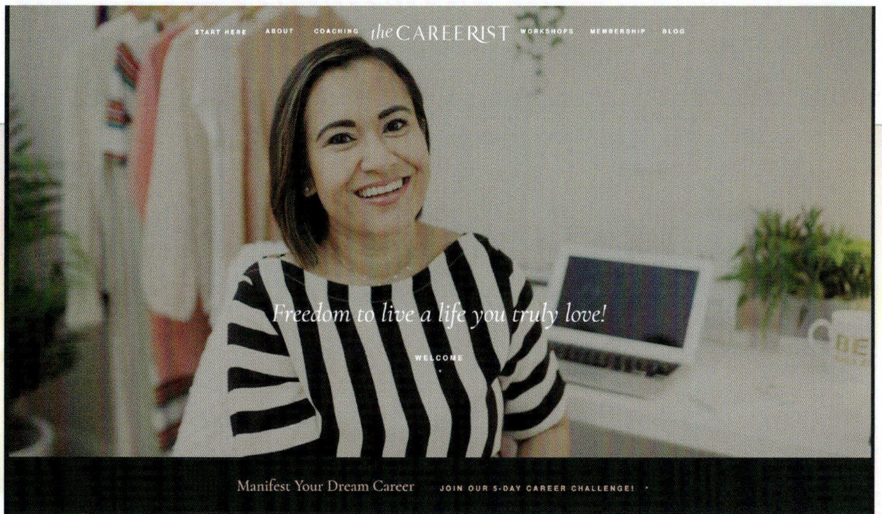

Manifest Your Dream Career JOIN OUR 5-DAY CAREER CHALLENGE! ›

HI, I'M

Natasha, Chief Careerist, Career Freedom Advocate, Executive Coach and Career Change Consultant.

I help ambitious women boldly embrace and embody change in their career + life. At The Careerist, our vision is to redefine career freedom, on OUR terms, through a feminist lens. We want to transform the way the world engenders women in the workplace, one conversation at a time.

MORE ON HOW I CAN HELP YOU ›

Careerist *ke • rie • rist | noun* SOMEONE WHO PRIDES THEIR PROFESSIONAL ADVANCEMENT AND CAREER AMBITIONS AS A TOP PRIORITY AND WHO WILL GO TO GREAT LENGTHS TO ACHIEVE SUCCESS FOR THEIR LIFE GOALS.

how can we help you today

Shall we collaborate on your future?

1:1 Career Coaching
TRANSFORMATIONAL COACHING

Corporate Workshops
BUSINESS + EXECUTIVE WORKSHOPS

Careerist Sisterhood
MEMBERSHIP SUBSCRIPTION

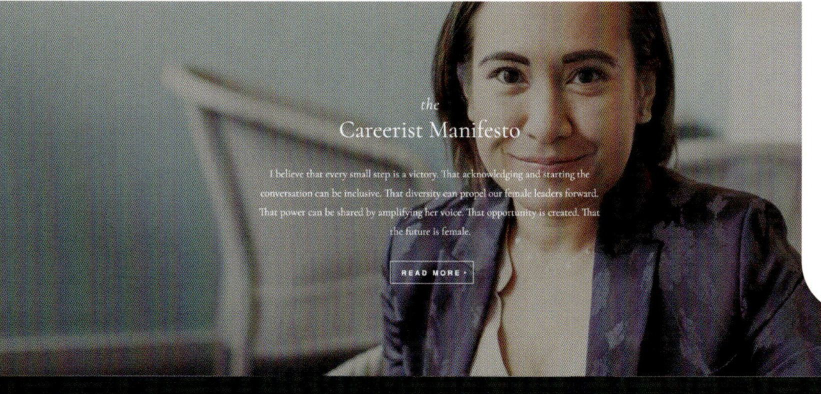

Serving you *brunch in bed* every Sunday – insights, inspiration, podcast updates + stories from our Careerist sisters.

First name
Last name
Here's my email

the CAREERIST

Freedom to live a life you truly love!

WELCOME

Manifest Your Dream Career

DIANA B & COMPANY

DIANAB.CO

Diana Walker of Diana B & Company is a boss to the core! With a bold, empowered site from Amber Crudup Branding Co., Diana's boutique finance firm for female entrepreneurs is sure to attract other strong women who are not afraid of investing in themselves and their business because they recognize value. Diana is confident with a dash of sass, and that's apparent through her use of a strong color palette, and fashionable branded photos. The site is attracting the right women and "it has made women more comfortable with opening up and being vulnerable about their money and challenging habits. They know they're not getting the typical stuffy corporate-like finance firm." There is definitely nothing stuffy about Diana or her online home!

DESIGNED BY

AMBER CRUDUP
AMBER CRUDUP BRANDING CO

AMBERCRUDUP.COM

COLORS

TYPEFACES

Open Sans Light

Cormorant Garamond Normal

Cormorant Garamond Italic

finances don't have to be overwhelming

Confused by all the finance & tax lingo? Need help organizing & getting your documents Tax Ready? Have you missed tax deadlines? We created an Income Tax Organizer to help you get allllllll of that together!

YES! I NEED THIS!

Hey girl, hey!

Marshawn Evans Daniels said it best: "Those who show up, go up." Here at Diana B & Company, we're committed to partnering with you so you can show up in the best way!!

In Business, in Finances, and in Life!

- ☑ *Get your time back*
- ☑ *Eliminate financial chaos & stress*
- ☑ *Make informed business decisions*
- ☑ *Put money back in your bag (aka: Lower Tax Bills)*
- ☑ *Grow your business, build wealth & legacy!*

MEET DIANA B WALKER

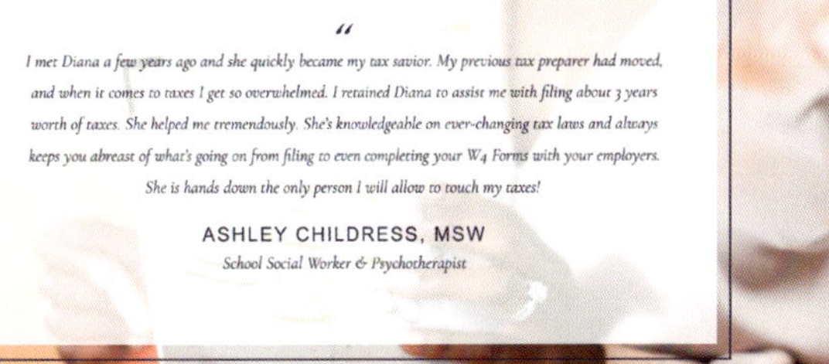

"

I met Diana a few years ago and she quickly became my tax savior. My previous tax preparer had moved, and when it comes to taxes I get so overwhelmed. I retained Diana to assist me with filing about 3 years worth of taxes. She helped me tremendously. She's knowledgeable on ever-changing tax laws and always keeps you abreast of what's going on from filing to even completing your W4 Forms with your employers. She is hands down the only person I will allow to touch my taxes!

ASHLEY CHILDRESS, MSW

School Social Worker & Psychotherapist

...for the busy, confused, & overwhelmed female entrepreneur...

DIANA B AND CO

offers an experience that will EXPOSE the root of your financial overwhelm & frustration, ENLIGHTEN you with financial knowledge, and EMPOWER you with financial clarity & confidence.

WE CALL THIS: THE "TRIPLE E" EXPERIENCE...

experience the difference

finances don't have to be overwhelming

Confused by all the finance & tax lingo? Need help organizing & getting your documents Tax Ready? Have you missed tax deadlines? We created an Income Tax Organizer to help you get allllllll of that together!

YES! I NEED THIS!

KARMA HILL PHOTOGRAPHY

KARMAHILL.COM

"A beach chic feel" can be used to describe all of Hawaii, but also to describe KarmaHill.com. Based out of paradise, aka Maui and Oahu, Karma Hill Photography is a team of talented and passionate photographers and editors. They specialize in stunning wedding photography and vibrant portraits. They are experts (over 2800 events photographed) at capturing beautiful sunsets and bright blue water, which is evident on their website. You can practically feel the ocean breeze, and breathe in the refreshing salty air as soon as you get on the site. This custom designed website by Brand & Brush perfectly captures the magic of Hawaii and is going to make all website visitors start dreaming of their next Hawaiian adventure. Captured by Karma Hill Photography, of course.

DESIGNED BY

JOHN & MEGAN FRANKS
BRAND & BRUSH

BRANDANDBRUSH.COM

COLORS

#4A4948

#FAB6B4

#589A96

#91BAC4

#F07A58

#FFCD6C

#F5F6F1

#FFFFFF

TYPEFACES

Fragile

Coco Gothic Light

COCO GOTHIC SMALLCAPS LIGHT

Greycliff Regular

Karma Hill
PHOTOGRAPHY TEAM

Karma Hill
PHOTOGRAPHY TEAM

BLOG

WEDDINGS

From elopements with no guests on the beach to lavish affairs, our photography team treats each wedding with love and passion for what we do,

VIEW WEDDINGS

PORTRAITS

We adore freezing time in the form of cherished portraits for our clients. We offer all kinds of portrait photography on Maui and Oahu.

VIEW PORTRAITS

MAGIC

Add a little magic to your portrait photography! Custom styled portrait packages are available, the only limit is your imagination!

VIEW MAGIC

Our Photography Style

WE CAPTURE AUTHENTIC EMOTION WITH THE BEAUTY OF THE ISLANDS AS YOUR BACKDROP.

Our Photography Style

WE CAPTURE AUTHENTIC EMOTION WITH THE BEAUTY OF THE ISLANDS AS YOUR BACKDROP.

Our images are bright, airy, dreamy and polished. Our professional editing staff hand edits each image for the most finished look. You will never see a beach goer in the background of your photos or a blemish on a beautiful face!

We are experts at natural light and use it as much as possible, our photographers are also trained in artificial light for those amazing sunset shots. Our Maui photography team is personable, friendly, professional yet relaxed putting you at ease in front of our cameras. We combine both posed and natural moments for a stunning photographic collection that represents you.

POSTS & RESOURCES

PORTRAITS
What To Wear

PORTRAITS
Top 10 Planning Tips

WEDDINGS
How To Stress Less On Your Wedding Day

WEDDINGS
Are We The Right Fit For You?

Our Philosophy

WHAT MAKES US DIFFERENT FROM OTHER MAUI PHOTOGRAPHERS?

Thanks for dropping by! I really want our team of professional Maui photographers to be a part of YOUR Maui experience. I like to think our photos speak for themselves, but I really want to give you the backstory on how they look so stunning and why I think our brand is so special.

P3 WEDDINGS & EVENTS

P3WEDDINGSANDEVENTS.COM

As a United States Army Veteran based out of Richmond, Virginia, it is easy to want to put Pearlice Diggs into a box. But then you get to her online home, and she instantly invites you to her "garden". This sweet place on the web is one you are going to want to stay at for awhile! It is a very inviting space that is timeless yet modern. The iris is the hallmark of her brand, in memory of her mother "who believed that everyday can be a celebration if we believe". So touching! Pearlice worked alongside her designer, Bernel Westbrook, to create her custom website that beautifully reflects her brand and passion for beauty and celebration - the perfect pairing.

DESIGNED BY

BERNEL WESTBROOK
BRANDED BY BERNEL

BRANDEDBYBERNEL.COM

COLORS

#FFFFFF

TYPEFACES

Cinzel Normal

Cormorant Infant Normal

Script

HOME MEET PEARLICE LOOKBOOK ACCOLADES THE EXPERIENCE CONTACT

WHERE EVERY FIBER OF YOUR EVENT MATTERS

"WE'RE HONORED TO CELEBRATE YOUR SPECIAL DAY"

OUR MISSION IS BUILT, CENTERED AND FOUNDED UPON YOU. THIS IS YOUR OPPORTUNITY TO CELEBRATE ONE OF LIFE'S BIGGEST MOMENTS! THEREFORE, WE'RE DEDICATED TO PLANNING, DESIGNING AND EXECUTING YOUR SPECIAL DAY WITH STELLAR SERVICE AND POLISHED VENDORS TO CREATE A SEAMLESS AND STRESS-FREE EVENT FOR YOU!

BROWSE THE LOOKBOOK

910-709-1597
PEARLICE@P3WEDDINGS.COM
7400 BEAUFONT SPRINGS DRIVE,
RICHMOND, VA, 23225, USA

FOLLOW US:

© P3 Weddings, Pearlice's Perfect Pair LLC. 2019. All rights reserved. | Designed by Branded by Bernel

KATE MANNELLA PHOTOGRAPHY

KATEMANNELLA.COM

With a mix of handwritten fonts and floral drawings, it is obvious that KateMannella.com is the online home of a creative with a refined eye. Working with Amanda Csaken from Brand Epiphany, both women put their heads together to create a site "designed to welcome new viewers and put them at ease." With classic design palettes, visitors navigate seamlessly through rustic farmlands, to downtown cityscapes. This mirrors the versatility of the fine art wedding photography of Kate Mannella Wedding Photography. And when Kate is not busy capturing her bride's intimate interactions with her groom, you can find her enjoying the farmers market, catching an Indian's game, or snuggling up to do some brand research on her coined "cozy sophistication."

DESIGNED BY

AMANDA CSAKAN
BRAND EPIPHANY

BRANDEPIPHANY.COM

COLORS

#212323

#58595B

#936275

#D6BDBD

#8B675E

#B18F7F

#FAF7F5

#FFFFFF

TYPEFACES

Jost Light

Cormorant Garamond Bold

Cormorant Garamond Normal

Cormorant Garamond Italic

HOME ABOUT THE EXPERIENCE KATE MANNELLA GALLERIES JOURNAL CONTACT

FINE ART WEDDING PHOTOGRAPHY

In the quiet mundane of everyday life is a sacredness waiting to be found. Your first sip of coffee in the morning, a friend's sweet embrace, a kiss that feels like a promise.... collect those wonders in your heart like little treasures. They were meant to be savored.

MEET KATE

I'm a fine art wedding photographer located in Cleveland, passionately serving couples in the Midwest and beyond. I believe our lives are worth celebrating, and my favorite way to celebrate is with photographs. Photos freeze moments with the people we love in time to savor forever. When we look back at photographs, the feelings we experienced are reignited over and over.

MORE ABOUT KATE

SAVOR EVERY MOMENT

My deepest aspiration for you is to create space. Space to be fully present and to savor this season. Time to relish each other and to reflect on what it truly means to embark on the sacred journey of marriage together.

ABOUT THE EXPERIENCE

KIND WORDS

"Working with Kate was an absolute joy. The photographs she took are a very meaningful piece of our wedding day that we will always cherish. We were overjoyed when we received our photographs and heard a multitude of compliments from family and friends praising her work. We have nothing but praise for Kate and recommend her to anyone in need of a professional and talented photographer."

LYNDSAY & LOGAN

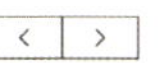

LET'S BE FRIENDS!

Get wedding inspiration, encouragement, gifts, and personal updates all in one place!

KATE MANNELLA

FINE ART WEDDING PHOTOGRAPHY

In the quiet mundane of everyday life is a sacredness waiting to be found. Your first sip of coffee in the morning, a friend's sweet embrace, a kiss that feels like a promise.... collect those wonders in your heart like little treasures. They were meant to be savored.

JOHN & SAMANTHA

JOHNANDSAMANTHA.CA

John and Samantha are a fun husband and wife photography team based out of Hamilton, Ontario, Canada. With 3 kids in tow, and having been in business for over 10 years, this couple really wants to capture meaningful moments for their clients. This is beautifully conveyed through their website, which started off with *Harlow*, a design by Buffalo Collective. Their candid, relaxed, and natural photographs take center stage. "We really wanted our website to feel like they were peeking into our living room... and we used a lot of written word to really communicate our style, vibe, and the philosophy behind our work." And their clients are loving this peek as their website has helped to convert visitors into clients and friends.

DESIGNED WITH

COLORS

#FFFFFF

TYPEFACES

Oswald Light

Brandon Grotesque

Raleway Normal

j+s

john + samantha

THIS IS YOUR STORY

PHOTO AND VIDEO BY
JOHN AND SAMANTHA BUTLER

We believe in marriage. It's what we're all about.

As a husband and wife team since 2009 with over 200 weddings behind us, we have the expertise to bring you truly stunning images thanks to a candid, relaxed, natural approach.

We want you to be free to live in the real moments, while we capture the fun, the emotions, the stories - as they truly happen.

THIS IS YOUR STORY

PHOTO AND VIDEO BY
JOHN AND SAMANTHA BUTLER

We believe in marriage. It's what we're all about.

As a husband and wife team since 2009 with over 200 weddings behind us, we have the expertise to bring you truly stunning images thanks to a candid, relaxed, natural approach.

We want you to be free to live in the real moments, while we capture the fun, the emotions, the stories - as they truly happen.

FEATURED
WEDDING STORY

PORTFOLIO

VIEW THE PORTFOLIOS: WEDDINGS VIDEOS COUPLES FAMILY LIFE

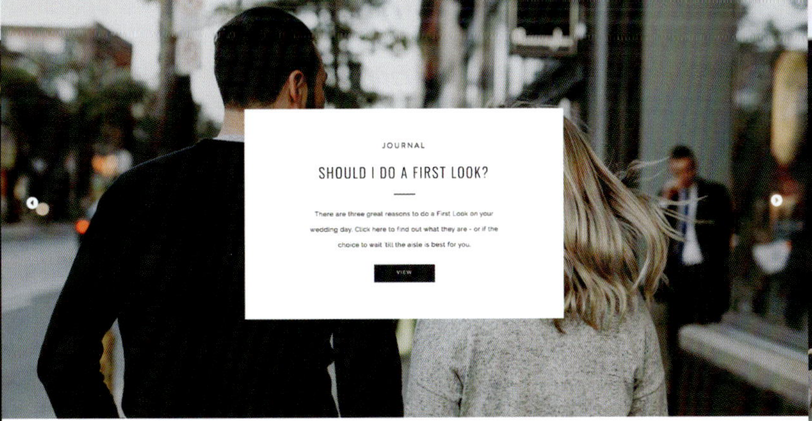

We're based in Hamilton, Ontario
Serving Toronto, the GTA, Niagara, Muskoka
and international destinations on request.

JOHN AND SAMANTHA BUTLER | [illegible] | HELLO@JOHNANDSAMANTHA.CA

HOW TO CREATE *THE PERFECT CONTACT PAGE* *FOR YOUR WEBSITE*

with ELIZABETH McCRAVY

Want to create your most effective and strategic contact page ever? If that sounds boring, hear me out. This *might* actually be one of the most important pages on your website. For service-based businesses, this page is what stands between someone learning about your services and starting the booking process with you. Let's make the most of it! Here are the top tips for an effective contact page.

1. *Your contact page should have a contact form and email address listed.*

These are the most important things on the page. You should always have a form AND your email address listed. Forms are easy, everyone typically has a form. But, do you have your email address listed for people who don't want to fill out your form? Or, for those who are contacting you about something that requires an email? Give users both options to contact you.

2. *Your contact form needs to ask these important questions*

- FIRST AND LAST NAME
- EMAIL ADDRESS
- WHAT IS THIS REGARDING?
- MESSAGE
- HOW THEY FOUND YOU

Ask the least amount of questions needed in order to get the user started in your process. The more questions you're asking, the less likely a visitor will fill out the form. Keep that in mind with every extra question you're choosing to add! No one wants to answer a thousand questions just to know your pricing or availability. And, many people filling out your form are doing so on a phone, which is not a great place to be answering 15+ questions. Limit your form to 5-8 questions.

3. *Avoid asking these questions on your main contact form.*

    - **PHONE NUMBER**
      This works if they are scheduling a call with you specifically, but don't do this on the main form. People don't want to be called unexpectedly.
    - **WHY THEY WANT TO WORK WITH YOU**
      This isn't about you. And at this point, they might not even know you yet. They are just getting started.
    - **WHAT THEIR BUDGET IS**
      Again, assume that they don't know you yet. This is too soon to be talking budgets.

    Although these questions can be really insightful, your initial contact form isn't the right place to be asking them. Save these types of questions for later in the process!

4. *Be sure to also include these important elements on your contact page.*

    - **EMAIL ADDRESS**
      Remember point #1! You will miss leads if you don't include this.
    - **PHOTO**
      Your image reminds them of the person behind the business name that they are specifically talking to, which is good to see while they are filling it out.
    - **LOCATION**
      Not your physical address, just where you live generally. People are curious!

5. *Consider additional content to engage your visitors.*

    - **OTHER WAYS TO CONNECT**
      Sign up for your email list, join your Facebook group, links to your podcast or YouTube channel, or any other places you engage your community.
    - **FREQUENTLY ASKED QUESTIONS**
      Just a few questions you're commonly asked.
    - **OFFICE HOURS**

Above all, focus on your viewers

When you're working on your website, always ask yourself, "How can I make this as easy as possible for my visitors?" and, "How can I make the visitor taking that first step simpler?!" Having a well-designed contact page is one way to do just that! Now, go change up your contact page! These simple tweaks really will help you grow your business and get more leads.

JENNIFER YOUNG PHOTOGRAPHY

JENNIFERYOUNG.CO

Jennifer Young is a Brooklyn based family portrait photographer who loves to document memories locally and beyond. Her online home is a custom website designed by Melissa Love of The Design Space Co., which boasts bright colors and fun photographs of the families she's served over the years. Born to a photographer, the passion for creating is in her blood and she enjoys making family sessions fun, lighthearted and full of jokes and giggles. Jen firmly believes in preserving legacies and recorded history, as well as the importance of showing up in photos as parents. Her relaxed and lighthearted style is reflected through the design on her website, creating a space that feels inviting and personal, and one that she gets a ton of compliments from.

DESIGNED BY

MELISSA LOVE
THE DESIGN SPACE CO.

THEDESIGNSPACE.CO

TYPEFACES

Summer Loving

Oswald Normal

Montserrat Bold

Montserrat Normal

Open Sans Normal

CONQUEROR ONE

CONQUEROR TWO

CLIENT LOGIN

HOME ABOUT PORTFOLIO INFO BLOG CONTACT

JENNIFER YOUNG PHOTOGRAPHY

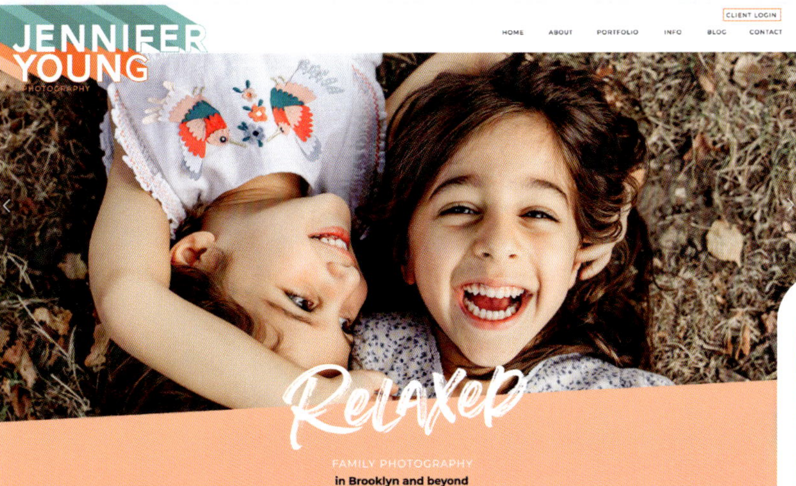

Relaxed

FAMILY PHOTOGRAPHY

in Brooklyn and beyond

THEY GROW SO

FAST

We hear this so often that it's become a cliché. And yet . . .

Our kids change so quickly before our eyes. We document our lives with our cell phones, but are those the family treasures that our grandkids and great-grandkids will find one day? Will those images ever be printed, framed, or preserved in an album?

As parents, we are not just guardians, caretakers, and educators.

WE ARE

memory keepers

We are family historians, and we are archivists.

IF YOU'RE HERE,

YOU PROBABLY ALREADY KNOW THIS.

I'm Jen, and I want to give you an easy and fun photography experience that captures the unique beauty of your family.

LET'S GET STARTED

Jen X

GET YOUR FREE WARDROBE GUIDE!

EMAIL ADDRESS

SUBMIT

HEY.

I WANT YOU TO #EXISTINPHOTOS

WHAT'S YOUR LEGACY?

FIND ME

I'm a Brooklyn-based family photographer available to work throughout the NYC area.
I can't wait to capture your family!

CONNECT

QUICK LINKS

CONTACT

BLOG

PORTFOLIO

JENNIFER YOUNG PHOTOGRAPHY

Relaxed

FAMILY PHOTOGRAPHY

in Brooklyn and beyond

THEY GROW SO

FAST

NICCI HUDSON

NICCIHUDSON.UK

Family photojournalism. Not two words that you always see together, but when you do, you know you are in store for some beautiful and meaningful images. With branding and logo help from the design gurus at The Design Space Co, Nicci managed to design an online home that is the perfect storefront for her powerful images. The minimalist black and white vibe makes an impact with pops of yellow. The carefully-paired fonts add even more character to this website that continues to draw its visitors in. The aesthetics aren't the only compelling parts of this site. Nicci, based in England, reminds us that family is at the center of our lives. She shares how important it is for moms to show up in their families' images. And she should know—as a busy and successful mom of four.

DESIGNED WITH

COLORS

#000000

#F8D33A

#636363

#DEB641

#353535

#05304F

#F5F5F5

#FFFFFF

TYPEFACES

Nixie One Normal

Monsterrat XLight

Monsterrat Regular

Monsterrat Bold

Just lovely

Sundays

ME
NU

NICCI HUDSON.

You hate cheesy family photos. You don't have time to get dressed up. Your toddler won't sit still. You have an awkward, forced smile in photos?

You want to preserve real memories of your family, as they are, real and raw - the tantrums, the belly laughs, and the emotions, a fraction of crazy, a little bit of loud and a whole lot of love - without the cheese - you want photos with real substance - y'know the ones that make you FEEL?

This is Family Photojournalism and that is exactly what I do.

MEET ME

ME
NU

NICCI HUDSON.

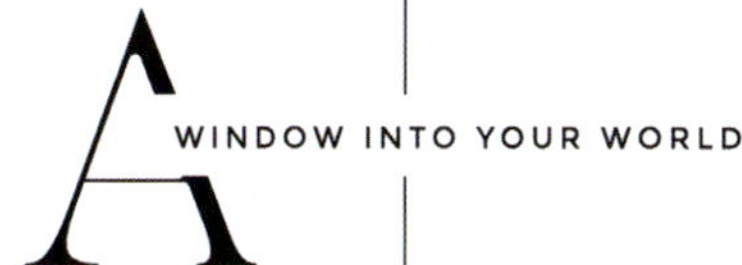

You hate cheesy family photos. You don't have time to get dressed up. Your toddler won't

TOAST OF LEEDS

TOASTOFLEEDS.CO.UK

Toast of Leeds is owned by Shelly, a wedding photographer based in Yorkshire. A born storyteller, Shelly began her career in journalism in a newsroom and now photographs luxury wedding stories for couples who love adventure and big moments. Her stunning website, custom designed by The Design Space Co., is a reflection of her unique, fun-loving personality. Her iconic photographs of the couples she's documented over the last thirty years truly highlight her talent and wisdom. Shelly's website boasts fun elements and surprises along the way that connect her with her couples before they ever meet. While she's based in Yorkshire, she loves to travel across the UK and Europe to photograph weddings and experience new adventures on her snowboard.

DESIGNED BY

MELISSA LOVE
THE DESIGN SPACE CO.

THEDESIGNSPACE.CO

TYPEFACES

Montserrat Bold

Nunito Normal

PARCEL

AND MOMENT
JUNKIES

Weddings go so fast. One minute you're walking down the aisle, and the next you're wondering where the day went. But don't worry, I'm here to capture all those tiny little moments - those crazy bridesmaids dancing, the groomsmen doing shots at the bar and your mum wiping away her happy tears, so that you don't miss a single minute.

AND MOMENT
JUNKIES

Weddings go so fast. One minute you're walking down the aisle, and

PO
RT
FO
LIO

AEVITAS WEDDINGS

AEVITASWEDDINGS.COM

With over 450 weddings under his belt, Henry Chen had many images to choose from to highlight on his website. And the images that greet you are vibrant, full of color and emotions. Henry is the amazing photographer behind Aevitas Weddings, and Sarah Blodgett of Digital Grace Design is the amazing designer behind this vibrant and stunning website. It is so perfectly organized, that you can really tell that Aevitas Weddings specializes in multicultural, and faith-centered weddings. There is a whole section, with accompanying blog posts, to specifically list out what can be expected at each cultural wedding. Whether you are Jewish, Vietnamese, Persian, Nigerian, or any mix of any culture—you can feel confident that Henry and his team know how to perfectly capture your day.

DESIGNED BY

SARAH BLODGETT
DIGITAL GRACE DESIGN

DIGITALGRACEDESIGN.COM

COLORS

#000000
#19191A
#636363
#747474
#969696
#D1A737
#ECEBE8
#FFFFFF

TYPEFACES

Didot

Cormorant Garamond Italic

Lato Normal

Lato Bold

REAL WEDDINGS BLOG YOUR WEDDING AEVITAS WEDDINGS CLIENT EXPERIENCE FAQS CONTACT

★★★★★ OVER 280 5 STAR REVIEWS

★★★★★ OVER 190 5 STAR REVIEWS

yelp

★★★★★ OVER 100 5 STAR REVIEWS

Google

KIND WORDS

"It was a pleasure to work with you from our engagement session to our wedding. You are very organized and professional, many guests gave me great feedback about you."

JOY & DAN
MARCH 7TH, 2020

SOUTHERN CALIFORNIA WEDDING PHOTOGRAPHER
SPECIALIZING IN MULTI-CULTURAL, FAITH, AND ETHNIC WEDDINGS

VIEW OUR REAL WEDDINGS

KIND WORDS

"As a professional photographer, I was anxious about finding one for my own wedding. I was so incredibly lucky to have found Henry. He was amazing and a helpful part of my

01 02 03 04 05 06 07 08 09 10

OVER 280 5 STAR REVIEWS

OVER 190 5 STAR REVIEWS

ALLIE ATKISSON IMAGING

ALLIEATKISSONIMAGING.COM

Allie and Tommy have not only incorporated their bold and intimate brand into their online home, but their fun personalities shine through there as well! With the help of Sarah at Digital Grace Design, the three put their heads together to customize a Buffalo Collective design for a "fresh yet classic and extremely relatable" website refresh. "The moment people reach our site they can immediately pick up on our vibe. People know who we are, what we stand for, and the product and experience we deliver before they even reach out to us." Coupling a natural color palette as a nod to their Arkansas roots, with fun branding photos, AllieAtkissonImaging.com finds the perfect balance between professional and relatable.

CUSTOMIZED BY

SARAH BLODGETT
DIGITAL GRACE DESIGN

DIGITALGRACEDESIGN.COM

COLORS

#1D1D1D
#1A2A3F
#8E999A
#B27050
#D8A94D
#EDE7E4
#F5F5F5
#FFFFFF

TYPEFACES

Cormorant Garamond Normal
Oswald Light
Raleway Normal
Excellent Signature

HOME ABOUT US SERVICES GALLERIES FAQ BLOG CONTACT CHECK YOUR DATE!

WELCOME

HAVE YOU HEARD WEDDING DAY GOES BY SO FRIGGIN FAST?

IT DOES. WE KNOW. WE'VE BEEN THERE.

Inevitably, over time you start to forget the little things about that day. The way your mom teared up when she saw you in your dress, the way his lip quivered as he held you close, the way your flowers encapsulated your personality; these are all things that gradually become a less vivid memory.

WELL, THEY WOULD HAVE, BUT NOW YOU HAVE US.

LEARN ABOUT OUR SERVICES

TOMMY & ALLIE

THE HUSBAND AND WIFE PHOTOGRAPHY TEAM DEDICATED TO MAKING OUR COUPLES FEEL LIKE TOP SHELF TEQUILA ON A TUESDAY.

The cool thing about us being your photographers is that we already have that freaky team-based-sixth-sense that married people tend to get over time. This always comes in handy on wedding day, but not so much when he senses how much I've spent on candles at Target. I've got you and Tommy's

ANDI BRAVO PHOTOGRAPHY

ANDIBRAVOPHOTOGRAPHY.COM

Andi Bravo Photography is a husband and wife fine art wedding photography and cinema team based in Oklahoma. Andi and Daniel fell in love while working together, and now document marriage stories for the couples they are so honored to serve. Their creative online home started off with *Henrietta* by Viva La Violet, and was customized by Digital Grace Designs. Their website is dedicated to beautiful galleries and love stories of the clients they've documented, with images that are romantic, soft and elegant. Their luxury brand compliments their gorgeous photographs, and future clients can't help but fall in love with them through their warm personal bios written by the person who loves them most, and knows them best - their spouse!

CUSTOMIZED BY

SARAH BLODGETT
DIGITAL GRACE DESIGN

DIGITALGRACEDESIGN.COM

COLORS

#333333
#595958
#868685
#C2C2C2
#BF989A
#D6BDBE
#E7D9DA
#FFFFFF

TYPEFACES

Bellefair Normal

Cormorant Garamond Italic

Work Sans Normal

Eternal Pen

Andi Bravo

PHOTOGRAPHY

ROMANTIC

AUTHENTIC

TIMELESS

tulsa, okc, dallas and anywhere

HOME MEET US THE DETAILS PORTFOLIO

Andi Bravo
PHOTOGRAPHY

FOR PHOTOGRAPHERS READ THE BLOG CONTACT

ROMANTIC

AUTHENTIC

TIMELESS

tulsa, okc, dallas and anywhere your sweet love takes you!

A WEDDING IS A GATHERING & CELEBRATION OF YOUR HEART'S DEEPEST DESIRE.

The wish to join your life with the one your soul adores. A wedding is more than just a childhood dream. We want your wedding to be remembered and treated that way, with the love that it deserves. Every moment documented for you to cherish for a lifetime.

we are andi & daniel, and we are both deeply in love with weddings and documenting them.

We have been wedding romantics and cupid cheerleaders for as long as we can remember. We love seeing the smiles on our crazy-in-love couples, adventuring with them, and converting gorgeous memories into photographs.

we'd be honored to capture each special moment of your wedding day.

VIEW OUR PHOTOGRAPHY OFFERINGS

VIEW OUR WEDDING FILMS

WOODWARD PARK ENGAGEMENT SESSION

ABBY & RYAN | UTICA SQUARE ENGAGEMENT,

RECENTLY ON THE BLOG

WEDDING AT THE MANSION AT WOODWARD

HISTORIC MANSION WEDDING AT WOODWARD

view all

SUBSCRIBE

subscribe to the newsletter to receive updates, exclusive wedding tips & more!

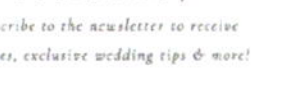

ANDI BRAVO PHOTOGRAPHY OFFERS FINE ART, CANDID, & ROMANTIC WEDDING PHOTOGRAPHY

based in tulsa, ok. available for travel.

HAVE QUESTIONS?

we'd love to help answer them!

SCHEDULE A CALL

back to top

SLOANE KETCHAM

SLOANEKETCHAM.COM

Sloane Ketcham is a woman who does hard things. She has built a business advocating and teaching entrepreneurs to do the same. So when it came to her online presence, she chose another hard worker - designer Elizabeth McCravy, to work with. Intentionally choosing brand images to fit the space, as well as a clear message of positivity, she is helping "women who want to turn their pain into purpose to purpose the calling on their lives." She even has a special page to share with her community and potential clients about her new book! Sloane, and her site, do such a great job at echoing this necessary message, that she simply titled her book *Beautiful Girl, You Can Do Hard Things*.

DESIGNED WITH

REESE MAYS BY ELIZABETH MCCRAVY

COLORS

#232423

#6898A5

#9EC6B3

#C5DBCE

#D8978C

#EAD5C4

#DDE2E2

#FFFFFF

TYPEFACES

Cabin Semi Bold

Rokkitt Normal

Butler Regular

Rahayu

Futura

xo, Sloane Ketcham

S × K

MENU

xo, Sloane Ketcham

GET THE TOOLS. JOIN YOUR TRIBE.
YOU WEREN'T MEANT TO DO THIS ALONE!

Tell Me More

Aloha!
I'm Sloane Ketcham

Believer, multi-passionate entrepreneur, mom, mountain mover & founder of the She Speaks Tribe. My mission in life is to help women courageously pursue the calling on their lives, through massive imperfect action, confidence, and a whole lot of faith!

Also obsessed with carbs (mostly pasta), Kim Crawford and I go way back, 90's music is my jam, and nothing happens before coffee!

TELL ME MORE

I'm Sloane Ketcham

Let's Do This Together

JOIN THE TRIBE

If you're a heart centered, ambitious boss lady, looking to launch, grow or accelerate your dream business, or you just want to change your life, cause you know you were #madeformore. Then come on in sister! We've been waiting for you!

MORE INFO PLS!

BLOG

Tips, tricks, and truths about faith, family, fortune, fashion, fitness & more from myself and our tribe of experts! Join us weekly for new content that'll have you saying, "Amen!"

SOUNDS LIKE FUN!

EVENTS

Our motto: High Tech, High Touch. We're a virtual tribe, who lounge in yoga pants and messy buns most days, but love happy hour and hugs too! We host meet-ups in person & virtually. Plus our She Speaks Hawaii Retreat! I can't wait to HUG yah!

SEE YOU SOON.

Praise Hands

JENNA C.

"Sloane helped me execute my plan with ease and grace! You can't go wrong with her!"

"If you're like me, you KNOW that you're supposed to grow your business online to reach your tribe. If you're like me, the HOW part scares you and you get stuck. Sloane and her team help us develop and execute the strategy. I love having a plan!"

WILD SPIRIT

WILDSPIRIT.CO

To visit the website of Wild Spirit Co. is to be whisked away to a world where Cassandra Lane is able to display her cute, quirky, nerdy side, and her high dexterity with words. Cassandra is a creative copywriter in Australia who has trained extensively in neuromarketing, consumer psychology, marketing strategy, and conversion copywriting. Her website, a unique adventure custom designed by Emma Troy, is an online journey unlike any other. And she wants to help other sites do the same. Since launching her site, she says her "conversions have increased dramatically and my reputation has grown as a powerful creative copywriter who gives brands irresistible personalities and websites undeniable presence," which is what her online home is, in a nutshell.

DESIGNED BY

EMMA TROY
EMMA TROY DESIGN

EMMATROY.COM.AU

COLORS

#231F20
#FEF1EB
#FAC5BD
#E42532
#587585
#E2E8E7
#FBFCFC
#FFFFFF

TYPEFACES

Raleway Normal

Raleway Bold

Playfair Display

Playfair Display Italic

WOO THEM WITH YOUR WORDS

Creative copywriting for adventurous entrepreneurs.

Hey, I'm Cass!

I'm your resident creative copywriter, wordy secret weapon, and hot chocolate sippin' sidekick.

I blend next-level word nerdery in the form of consumer psychology, neuromarketing strategy and creative storytelling for personality-driven **words that woo** and **copy that converts.**

I'm here to extract your raw genius and translate it into captivating **web copy**, **content marketing** and **sales funnel copy** that illuminates your brilliance, articulates your value and sets you up for serious success.

MEET YOUR WORD NERD

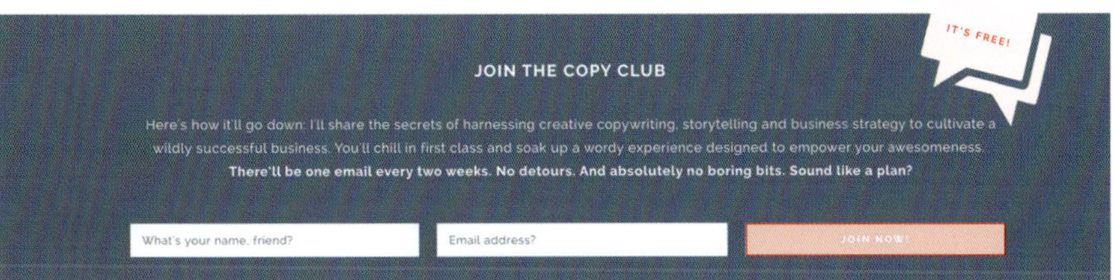

Your adventure starts here.

GRAB YOUR PASSPORT, PACK A BAG (DON'T FORGET SNACKS!) AND PREPARE TO GO ON THE WORDY TRIP OF A LIFETIME

01

Transform your online home

into a digital destination your dream peeps can't wait to explore.

CREATIVE WEBSITE COPYWRITING

02

Captivate and convert

with powerful email and content marketing sales funnels.

SALES FUNNEL COPYWRITING

WOO THEM WITH YOUR WORDS

Creative copywriting for adventurous entrepreneurs.

Hey, I'm Cass!

BELLE BODAS EVENTS

BELLEBODASANDEVENTS.COM

Braelynn is the heart and soul behind Belle Bodas Events. Through planning her own destination wedding in Mexico, Braelynn realized her passion and talent for creating events that are intentionally designed and thoughtfully curated for the clients she serves. With a custom website designed by Foil and Ink, Braelynn's life, work, and passions were the inspiration for the site. And as a non-traditionalist, her new site is speaking more to her dream clients, as well as organizing their inquiry process "because our couples now show up educated with our timeline and feel more confident booking." Braelynn currently lives in Utah with her husband Cody and their dog, Bear, while planning dream weddings for her couples all over the world.

DESIGNED BY

JACKI MILLER
FOIL & INK

FOILANDINK.COM

COLORS

#000000

#A98146

#B96156

#D9A893

#F0D8C9

#F6F1EB

#FFFFFF

TYPEFACES

Marbre Sans

Montserrat Normal

Montserrat Semi Bold

Hola Amor...

BELLE BODAS EVENTS BRINGS EXPERTISE, PASSION, AND EXPERIENCE TO THE WEDDING INDUSTRY.

Learn About Our Journey

HERE

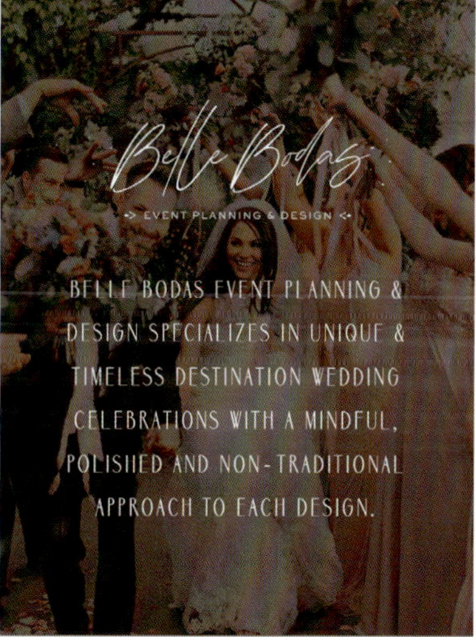

View Our Work

THE LAUREN STYLE

THELAURENSTYLE.COM

An expert in style and strategy, Lauren, of The Lauren Style, is a brand photographer and strategist. Helping business owners around the world tell their stories and elevate their products through styled imagery is her jam. Her custom Foil and Ink website, which started with the *Carpe Diem* template, is the home to her multifaceted business, with a very fun and inspirational magazine vibe. The video at the first opening of her site draws you in, and the fresh copy keeps you reading. Visitors are in for a treat at every turn on her website. She's recently been featured in some of style's top publications as a small-town girl from Oregon and is now located in Arizona and serving businesses worldwide.

DESIGNED BY

JACKI MILLER
FOIL & INK

FOILANDINK.COM

COLORS

#000000

#796A38

#F7F3EE

#CB9587

#91504E

#EFE2D5

#FFFFFF

TYPEFACES

Playfair Display Italic

Oswald Light

Open Sans Light

MENU

the Lauren style.

Welcome To The Lauren Style.

ARE YOU READY TO TRANSFORM YOUR BUSINESS...
AND CHANGE YOUR LIFE?

I'm a photographer and brand strategist helping business owners elevate their products through styled imagery.

Corner Of The Web!

I'm a small-town girl from a big family, born and raised in Oregon. I love bulldogs, baking, and beautiful things, and I'll never, ever say no to hearing a good joke. I've had a camera in my hands for as long as I can remember, and big dreams even longer than that. That's why I knew that working a desk job was not for me. I'm an expert at content and branding strategy, creating and styling beautiful photoshoots, and helping you bring your image and brand to the next level.

LEARN MORE ABOUT ME!

TRANSFORM YOUR IMAGES
WITH ONE SIMPLE CLICK

Download My Free Mobile Preset By Clicking The Link Below

GIVE ME THE PRESET

I'm Not Your Average Photographer.

Wanna know a secret? Here it is: photographers are kinda a dime a dozen. I bet you could find someone with a DSLR camera to take your photo with your eyes closed.

Here's what sets me apart: I'm obsessed with using my photographs to bring my clients and their businesses to the NEXT LEVEL. I'm an expert when it comes to style and strategy and making YOU stand out of the crowd. But most of all, I'm obsessed with helping people become the BOSS they were meant to be.

Check Out My Photography Below

Welcome To The Lauren Style.

ARE YOU READY TO TRANSFORM
YOUR BUSINESS...
AND CHANGE YOUR LIFE?

I'm A Photographer And Brand Strategist Helping Business Owners Elevate Their Products Through Styled Imagery.

I DO EVENTS BY NICOLE

IDOEVENTSBYNICOLE.COM

"Our brand is designed for the bride who wants to think out of the box, loves to have fun, and wants to create a completely unforgettable experience for all of her guests." And that's exactly what website visitors get as well. Nicole, the wedding planner behind this website, started with *The Erin* template by Gillian Sarah, and customized it so that it would truly reflect her and her brand. It is fun with a touch of luxury and intimacy. As a hard working boss mom, you know that she is all about efficiency and good work. Which is why she loves her new site, as it helps her to get new leads, and it's a platform for brides and vendors to see her work.

DESIGNED WITH

THE ERIN GILLIAN SARAH

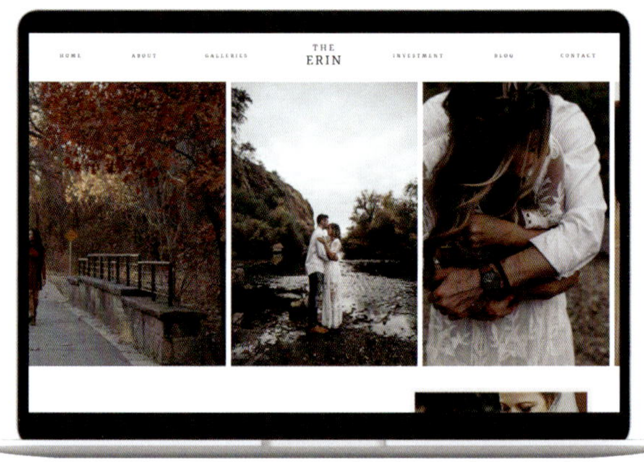

COLORS

#002B5C

#83A5DB

#C7E3F2

#ECEEF4

#EBEDF4

#E8E8E8

#A9A9A9

#FFFFFF

TYPEFACES

Yrsa Light

Yrsa Normal

Zeyada Normal

HOME MEET NICOLE LOVE NOTES i/do EVENTS BY NICOLE GALLERIES SERVICES CONTACT

MAKE YOUR DAY UNFORGETTABLE

WELCOME

Thank you for visiting our website!

At I Do Events by Nicole, we strive to provide our couples with the ultimate planning and wedding experience. We understand that no two couples or events are the same. So let us curate your event to fit your needs and tell the story of your love!

FIND OUT MORE

MAKE YOUR DAY UNFORGETTABLE

WELCOME

Thank you for visiting our website!

At I Do Events by Nicole, we strive to provide our couples with the ultimate planning and wedding experience. We understand that no two couples or events are the same. So let us curate your event to fit your needs and tell the story of your love!

GALLERIES

SERVICES

CONTACT

704.790.9133

nicole@idoeventsbynicole.com

Charlotte, NC

HOME GALLERIES

MEET NICOLE LOVE NOTES

SERVICES CONTACT

DESIGNED BY GILLIAN SARAH

LISHA HILL STUDIOS

LISHAHILLSTUDIOS.COM

With sweet sophistication, LishaHillStudios.com has achieved the right balance of images and narrative for an amazing site. A simple "About" page allows the viewer to know that their wedding day will be about them. After graduating with degrees in Photography & Communication + Information Design, Lisha became serious about capturing and recording people's stories. In fact, she refers to herself as a "storyteller" rather than a "photographer", ensuring the spotlight falls on her clients and their story. Customizing a design by Gillian Sarah allowed Lisha to create an easy, self-flowing website that is minimalistic. And no matter which galleries one chooses to venture through, visitors will see themselves reflected in these couples and hoping Lisha will be able to tell their story in her own special way.

DESIGNED WITH

THE RYANN BY GILLIAN SARAH

COLORS

#CAB37A

#18201D

#181818

#696E61

#FFFFFF

#87745B

TYPEFACES

Playfair Display

Mate Normal

Bentham Normal

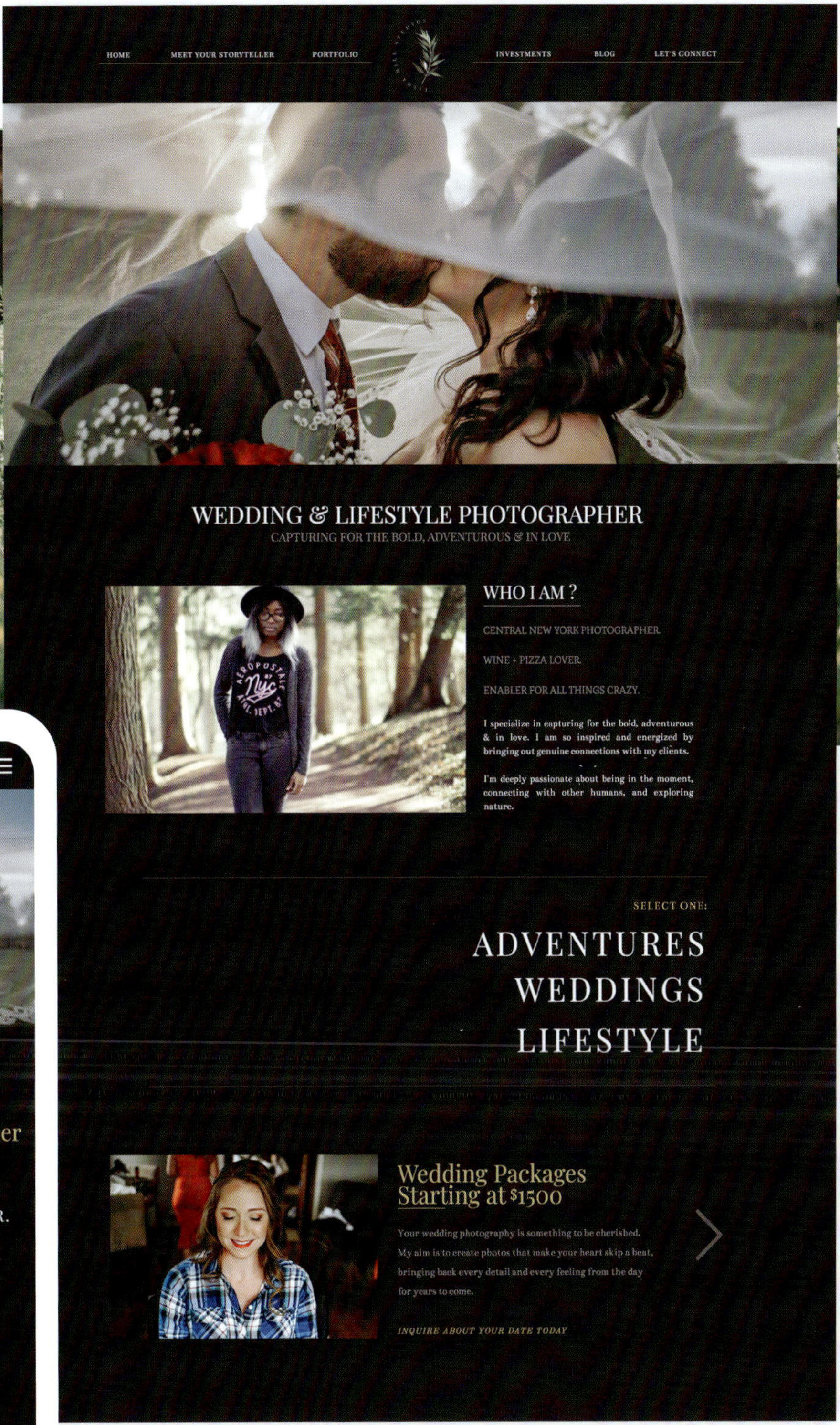

HOME MEET YOUR STORYTELLER PORTFOLIO INVESTMENTS BLOG LET'S CONNECT

WEDDING & LIFESTYLE PHOTOGRAPHER

CAPTURING FOR THE BOLD, ADVENTUROUS & IN LOVE

WHO I AM ?

CENTRAL NEW YORK PHOTOGRAPHER.

WINE + PIZZA LOVER.

ENABLER FOR ALL THINGS CRAZY.

I specialize in capturing for the bold, adventurous & in love. I am so inspired and energized by bringing out genuine connections with my clients.

I'm deeply passionate about being in the moment, connecting with other humans, and exploring nature.

SELECT ONE:

ADVENTURES

WEDDINGS

LIFESTYLE

Wedding Packages Starting at $1500

Your wedding photography is something to be cherished. My aim is to create photos that make your heart skip a beat, bringing back every detail and every feeling from the day for years to come.

INQUIRE ABOUT YOUR DATE TODAY

RACHEL HAYLIE

RACHELHAYLIE.CO

Rachel, of Rachel Haylie Photography, has a huge heart for her clients that influences every aspect of her business. So when it came to customizing her website design from Gillian Sarah, she of course, looked to them for inspiration. "I used their laughter and joy all over my website, along with clean and simple colors so the focus would be on the photographs themselves." While some creatives want their online home to be all things to all people, Rachel really wanted to keep her site classic and light so as not to overwhelm her ideal clients. With a focus on candid imagery and her "why", couples all over Oregon will be asking Rachel to reserve their wedding dates years in advance.

DESIGNED WITH

THE YASMIN BY GILLIAN SARAH

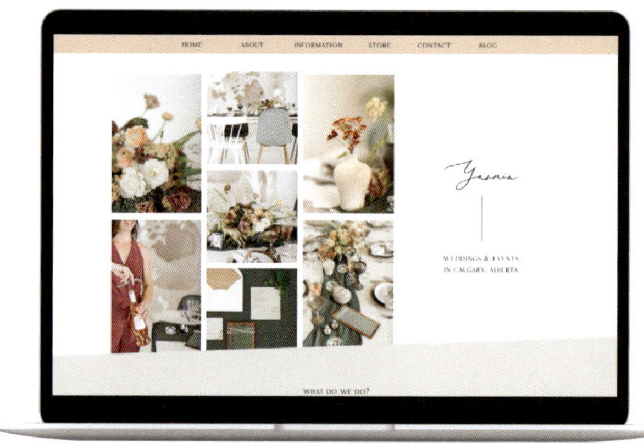

COLORS

#191919

#CEC8B6

#E4E2E3

#DFD5CB

#E7E7E7

#E3E0DB

#FFFFFF

TYPEFACES

Hunter

Maison de Fleur

Old Standard TT Normal

HEY THERE, I'M

Rachel

I'll never forget the wonder and thrill I embodied when presented with the challenge of constructing a cardboard pinhole camera, developing its film in the darkroom, and fashioning prints by hand. Though this was merely an introductory high school photography course, I knew I'd landed on something meaningful, something profoundly resonant, and something which would remain in my life for the long haul.

HOME | ABOUT | INFORMATION | CONTACT | BLOG (COMING SOON)

Rachel HAYLIE

CANDID, COLORFUL & LIGHTHEARTED

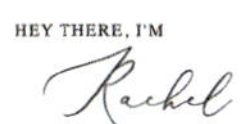

WELCOME, I'M SO GLAD YOU'RE HERE

My name is Rachel and as you can see photography has completely won my heart. (...Along with bunnies and the ocean!) I'm 26, full of laughter, playfulness and I've been blessed enough to have been working with bride and grooms for 6 years now. Wedding days are filled with a myriad of wonderful emotions, fleeting moments and hearty laughs. I am grateful to act as the eyes and the heart behind the lens, to capture love stories and to potentially work by your side to help create heirlooms worth treasuring.

As an artist, I see the ordinary as extraordinary. I instinctively find newness in my daily surroundings. To normalize what's exceptional, to "adjust" to routine, is to deprive the soul. Beauty -- as I see it -- is plentiful each day. Birds fluttering and dancing in front of a pale grey sky, clouds floating past in warm hues of pastel, beams of glimmering sunlight bursting through to graze the forest floor – witnessing such phenomena brings me joy and tremendous inspiration. I approach couples with the same enthusiasm and attentiveness. I strive to unveil and record these unique, timeless attributes as I focus on the candid moments that genuinely portray the two of you as a couple. By lacing natural light with love and laughter, a beautiful story unfolds -- and I feel deeply privileged that it's my task to capture this.

HEY THERE, I'M

Rachel

I'll never forget the wonder and thrill I embodied when presented with the challenge of constructing a cardboard pinhole camera, developing its film in the darkroom, and fashioning prints by hand. Though this was merely an introductory high school photography course, I knew I'd landed on something meaningful, something profoundly resonant, and something which would remain in my life for the long haul.

During this era of personal discovery, my mother shared a relic of her decades-past life with me - a vintage suitcase plastered with tattered stickers, each emblazoned with names of bands from before I was born. To my astonishment, I learned that my mother – as introverted, conservative and gentle as she is – once thrived as a photographer for metal concerts.

Yet another seed planted within my core! Soon, I eagerly began collecting diverse camera types, experimenting with their possibilities, and upturning their once-mysteries. And this fascination hasn't escaped me; rather, it has grown. To carve a livelihood from my highest passion is an honor, and to connect with others throughout the experience truly amplifies this delight. I am truly filled with joy when capturing weddings or families and I hope that my clients can see that when being photographed by me!

STEPHANIE & TREVOR
Ashland, Oregon

DANIELLE & CHAZ
Boise, Idaho

CARLIE & JEFF
Portland, Oregon

Designed by Gillian Sarah

LINDSAY ALISE PHOTOGRAPHY

LINDSAYALISEPHOTOGRAPHY.COM

There is a simple difference that sets Lindsay apart. As a pediatric nurse, she saw first hand the need to capture every cherished moment. As an extension of her photography, Lindsay's website pulls you into each enchanting scroll. Visitors will quickly learn that there is nothing dry about this Arizona photographer's images. Through her About page, we learn what her well-designed website has hinted at. "I am a sucker for warm colors, radiating sunlight flare, mixed patterns, and emotional connections. If that's what you want out of your session, I'm your girl." By using Jessica Gingrich's *Westlake* design, Lindsay was able to make the exact design changes she wanted to achieve an inviting online storefront that any visitor will feel at home on.

DESIGNED WITH

WESTLAKE BY JESSICA GINGRICH

COLORS

#000000

#7E7E7E

#FFF2F0

#EFE9E8

#FFDDD4

#DBDBDB

#BABABA

#FFFFFF

TYPEFACES

Roboto Condensed Normal

Roboto Condensed Italic

Playfair Display Normal

HOME
ABOUT
PORTFOLIO
KIND WORDS
DETAILS
CONTACT

Lindsay Alise
PHOTOGRAPHY

LINDSAY ALISE PHOTOGRAPHY
BASED IN PHOENIX, ARIZONA

READ THE *journal*

WHO WE ARE
and what we love

Lindsay Alise Photography is one of Arizona's best Newborn and Family Photographer serving Phoenix and surrounding areas.

We offer in-studio Newborn Sessions with custom props and hand-knit outfits to choose from. Our Maternity and Family Sessions are available on location at some of the most breathtaking spots in Arizona.

Every session is styled to suit your family and tell your story. From the time of your inquiry, to the delivery of your images, your experience will be flawless.

Check us out on instagram @lindsayalisephotography

GALLERIES
view our work

MATERNITY

NEWBORN

FAMILY

maternity
INVESTMENT
STARTS AT $450

PACKAGE INCLUDES:

+ One hour of on-location shooting
+ Sunset session
+ Use of maternity gowns
+ Style guidance and pre-session phone consultation
+ Immediate family included
+ 30 digital images delivered via online gallery
+ $100 deposit to secure session date

family/milestone
INVESTMENT
STARTS AT $450

PACKAGES INCLUDES:

+ One hour of on-location shooting
+ Sunrise or sunset session options
+ Style guidance and pre-session phone consultation
+ Immediate family included (up to five). Additional family for $25 per person
+30 digital images delivered via online gallery
+$100 deposit to secure session date

newborn
INVESTMENT
STARTS AT $500

PACKAGE INCLUDES:

+ Two hour studio session
+ Access to all studio outfits, backdrops, props, and wraps
+ Pre-session phone consultation to style and design session
+ Images with parents and siblings included
+ 15 digital images delivered via online gallery
+ $100 deposit to secure session
+ Best time to schedule is 2-3 months prior to delivery

HEY BEAUTIFUL,
my name is Lindsay

Hi there! I'm Lindsay. I'm a Pediatric Nurse and creative artist with a passion for Newborn & Family Photography. My biggest desire is to serve families through my work in the hospital and as a photographer.

MENU

Lindsay Alise

WHO WE ARE
and what we love

Lindsay Alise Photography is one of Arizona's best Newborn and Family Photographer serving Phoenix and surrounding areas.

We offer in-studio Newborn Sessions with custom props and hand-knit outfits to choose from. Our Maternity and Family Sessions are available on-location at some

XAYLI BARCLAY

XAYLIBARCLAY.COM

Xayli Barclay wanted to give her website visitors "a light-hearted and enjoyable experience", and that's exactly what you get while perusing her site by Jessica Gingrich. As a visual content creation coach, and an influential YouTuber who hails from Trinidad, Xayli commands your attention. Her style, her exuberant personality, and her content are all perfectly displayed in a modernly-retro way. Xayli still isn't where she wants to be, but is excited about how far she has come. And she is passionate about getting others to where they want to be as well! Thanks to her rebranded website, she is able to "connect with my audience and turn them into dear friends and customers".

DESIGNED WITH

ERIN BORDEAUX BY JESSICA GINGRICH

COLORS

#000000

#192533

#FFFFFF

#C5C5C5

#92B0C0

#FF5C5C

#DEE7EC

#F5F5F5

TYPEFACES

Rufina Normal

Lato Normal

Montserrat Normal

my font

WANT TO LEARN HOW TO CREATE BETTER VIDEOS FOR YOUR COURSES?

>>> GET YOUR FREE GUIDE

XayLi Barclay

MENU

VIDEO CONTENT IS....

The most powerful way for you to tell your story, build your brand, show your expertise and sell your products and services. Teaching you How To Start, Create & Dominate Smart & Strategic video content is my specialty!

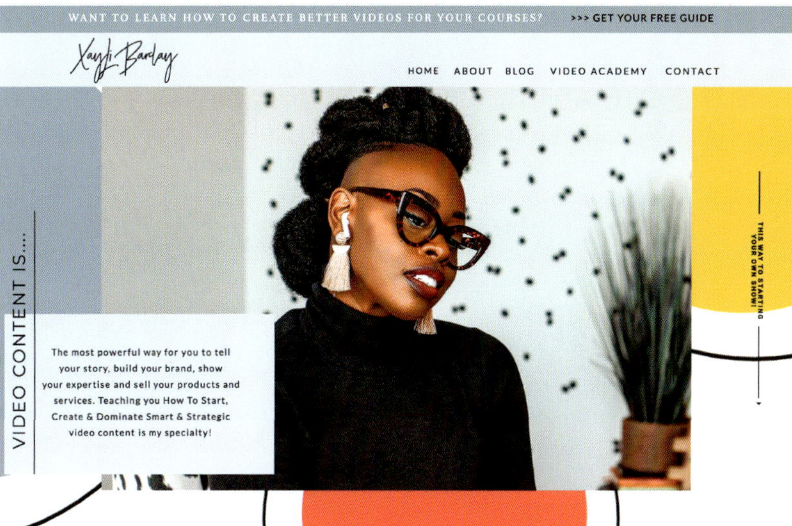

Are you a video newbie? video star? or a video pro?

Infopreneur, Course Creator, Online Business Owner, Freelancer?

Video marketing is an essential part of creating a genuine connection with your growing audience! Whether you are, creating, marketing, or selling your products and services, video content is the best way to do it!

HAVE YOU BEEN NERVOUS ABOUT CREATING VIDEOS?

GRAB THIS BUNDLE

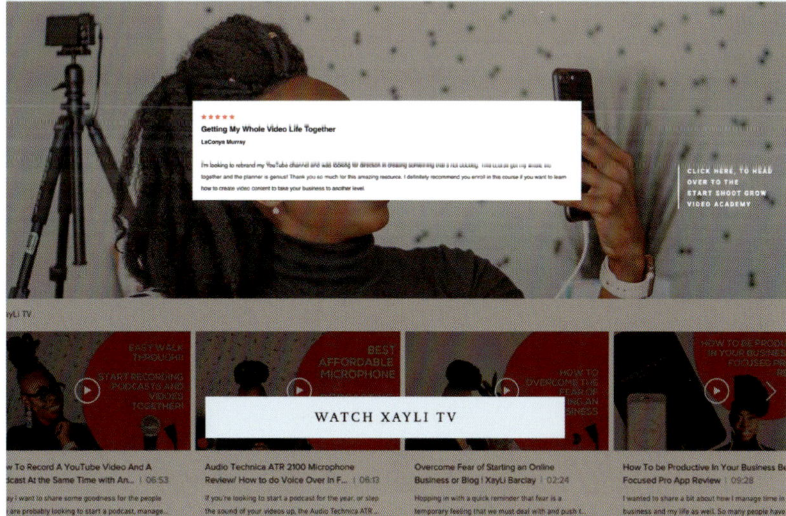

join us

THE START, SHOOT, GROW VIDEO FOR BUSINESS ACADEMY

LEARN MORE

AMANDA DONAHO

AMANDADONAHO.COM

The key to a really well-made online home is finding the correct balance of graphic elements to highlight the creative's services. By enlisting Kaleigh Turner Creative for a full brand and site overhaul, AmandaDonaho.com has the attention to detail to set the stage for booking her ideal client. Her site balances an "effortless, intimate, and refined" design element that frames her timeless, classic work. The roll-over feature on her image gallery whisks you from one portrait to another, only stopping to take in a brief description of where each click will take you next. Whether it's weddings, engagements, branding sessions, or even her travel print shop, this online storefront is deceptively deep. Which is perfect for turning visitors into clients!

DESIGNED BY

KALEIGH TURNER
KALEIGH TURNER CREATIVE

KALEIGHTURNERCREATIVE.COM

COLORS

#000000
#333333
#B2B2B2
#E1E1E1
#F3E7DE
#FDFDFD
#FFFFFF

TYPEFACES

Montserrat Light Italic

TROYE

Rachel

PORTFOLIO

TELLING YOUR *story*

Finding an emotional connection with the images your wedding photographer takes as well as their personality, is so important. In order to craft beautiful imagery together, it's essential for the couple to feel comfortable with the person they're trusting to tell their love story via photos. I'd love to talk more with you, or connect over a glass of red.

LET'S CHAT >

STAY UP TO DATE...
GET THE LATEST

EMAIL ADDRESS SUBSCRIBE

BROWSE	ELSEWHERE	BUSINESSES	SUBSCRIBE	VISIT THE BLOG
PORTFOLIO	FACEBOOK	BRAND SESSIONS	WEDDING TIPS	
ABOUT	INSTAGRAM	ILLUMINARE	NEWSLETTER	
CONTACT		COURSES		

J. MIKADO PHOTOGRAPHY

JMIKADO.COM

According to Jackie of J. Mikado Photography, type A personalities are getting a bad rep, but they should be given credit for helping her to be successful. “My perfectionism will be to your benefit. I fully support my Type A personality… there is nothing wrong with dotting all the i’s and crossing all the t’s.” Fortunately, working with Kaleigh Turner Creative, a new brand and website were created with the same attention to detail. Using the cherry blossom throughout her site pays homage to Jackie’s Japanese heritage. The floral images are modern and romantic to mirror and reinforce the tone of her images. In turn, those modern brides looking for detail-oriented photographers will surely be contacting her.

DESIGNED BY

KALEIGH TURNER
KALEIGH TURNER CREATIVE

KALEIGHTURNERCREATIVE.COM

COLORS

TYPEFACES

Chloe

Cormorant Garamond Bold Italic

Cormorant Garamond Medium

Montserrat Light

Home
About
Portfolio

J . M I K A D O

photography

The Experience
Blog
Contact

Nashville, Tennessee Wedding + Engagement Photographer
Available For Worldwide Travel

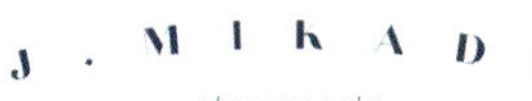

Nashville, Tennessee

LOVE IS IN THE DETAILS

We all have a story behind our love. Was it a chance encounter? A blind date? Friendship that turned into more?

The you-ness can be found in the details. It's in the way that you crinkle your nose when you laugh. The goodnight kiss right before you fall asleep. Filling up your partners car with gas when you borrow it. These details are everything in a relationship, because they remind us why we fell in love in the first place.

Your wedding will be a whole day of all the details that will represent who you are as a couple. I want to share my passion for all the small and big moments with you.

WELL HELLO.

I'M JACKIE

Hey Y'all, I'm a Wedding Photographer based in Nashville, Tennessee.

If you know me and love me, you'll know that I always order the same drink at Starbucks: Grande white chocolate mocha with nonfat milk, hold the whip. You'll also know that favorite store is Target, I'm always a fan of a good excel spreadsheet, and I'm fascinated with my Japanese heritage.

Over the years I have photographed well over 150 weddings and still loving experiencing each special moment. With a heart for service, I spend my days gushing over my clients making them the center of my universe. My promise to you is to laugh with you, cry with you, and always dance my heart out, awesome bad dance move in all.

More About Me ⟶

THE EXPERIENCE

If you haven't guessed it already...I'm all about the details. It's more than capturing a pretty picture. It's going the extra mile to make your dreams a reality. I strive to be a calming presence and the most worry-free part of your day so you can spend it focusing on what matters most. It's in capturing the real authentic moments and little nuances that go unnoticed.

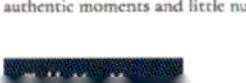

DANIELLE IRELAND

DANIELLEIRELAND.COM

The first image that pops on the screen is a lovely and friendly image of Danielle Ireland, mental health therapist and speaker extraordinaire, that truly makes you feel like you know her and can trust her. Working with Kristin of K Design Co., her new website and brand are able to clearly reflect who Danielle is and how she hopes to help others. "I now have a website and brand that is aspirational and can grow with me. It makes me want to work harder. This experience has given me more confidence to introduce myself as a professional. My website represents the type of work I hope to put out in the world - warm, sincere, and of the highest quality."

DESIGNED BY

KRISTIN PRUIS
K DESIGN CO.

THEKDESIGNCO.COM

COLORS

#C2965A

#F5D9CC

#F7F7F7

#E0E9E8

#8CABB0

#304552

#333333

#FFFFFF

TYPEFACES

Crimson Text Normal

Quickbrush

Quattrocento Sans Normal

Quattrocento Sans Italic

Quattrocento Sans Bold

Danielle
IRELAND

SUBSCRIBE

You want to live your best life...

but stuff's getting in the way

Together we can clear the clutter to add purpose and freedom to your life.

SPEAKER REEL ▸

LET'S WORK TOGETHER

One-on-One
THERAPY

Maybe you're struggling with a particular issue like depression, anxiety, or overwhelm. Or perhaps you're just not where you thought you'd be by now. No matter what's on your heart, I'd love to come alongside you in a one-on-one therapy session.

Keynote
SPEAKING

Expect depth and expertise drawn from my education and mental health licensing, but my performer's heart is what really lights up the stage. Enlightening and entertaining audiences brings me joy as I inspire others to seek wholeness.

Group & Team
WORKSHOPS

Let's bring your people together to tackle some of life's most meaningful topics. From empathy to self-forgiveness, social media to connection, my workshops cover relevant material and give participants powerful, actionable insights.

LEARN MORE

Danielle
IRELAND

You want to live your best life...

but stuff's getting in the way

Together we can clear the clutter to add purpose and freedom to your life.

SPEAKER REEL ▸

PRAISE

Danielle is a gifted speaker. Her authenticity and vulnerability shine as she guides women through exercises to be the best version of themselves.

- Julie Kratz, Speaker & author -

FREE QUIZ

Are you using social media, or is it using you?

Take my quiz to find out.

Is social media like a bad boyfriend? Your relationship with social can delight or drain. Let's see where you stand.

TAKE THE QUIZ

HOT OFF THE BLOG

What's my Netflix Binge Trying to Tell ...

Have you ever caught yourself binging a TV show and noticed the crum-covered blanket crater you've created on your couch? Or have you ever told yourself before turning on the TV, "I'll just watch one or two

HOW TO GET HIGH QUALITY CLIENT TESTIMONIALS

with JESSICA GINGRICH

Client testimonials are essential for growing your business.

Client testimonials provide your business with credibility and give your potential clients both a sense of security and trust, as well as confidence that your services will actually help them like they help others. If you are just starting out it can be hard to get your first few clients without any testimonials or social proof so I often recommend offering your services for free or discounted in return for a great testimonial that you can display on your website.

But how do you actually get high quality reviews that will lead to more clients and bookings?

You'd think it's as simple as asking a client, "Hey, so and so! Would you mind writing a testimonial for me?" and then waiting for them to send you a pretty generic (albeit super kind and sincere), "Jessica was awesome to work with. She was responsive and I love the website she created for me!"

This is awesome to hear, don't get me wrong, but honestly when your potential clients see that, all they are getting out of it is that you are a good person or a good designer. But those types of testimonials are a dime a dozen and don't make an impact on new potential clients.

They aren't seeing HOW you are going to help them other than the fact that you're capable of creating something beautiful, just like your competition. I'm a big fan of the Storybrand framework by Donald Miller and his method of marketing really focuses on your client's story.

To stand out from the crowd and really speak to your dream client, reach out to some of your past clients and ask them to answer the following questions:

1 What were you struggling with before working with me or using my product?

2 What made you decide to go with my services or product instead of a competitor?

3 How did you feel after our process was complete? How has your life or your business benefited from my services or product?

Those three questions will guide your past clients to provide you answers that you can use that potential clients want to know as well!

Knowing your client's pain points before purchasing your service or product is crucial in order to start speaking to your customer's story. This allows you to focus on the psychological or emotional pains more than the physical need.

Were they feeling frustrated, overwhelmed, or lost on how to do something? Were they lacking confidence, struggling with self-value, or failing to book their own clients?

Chances are your next client will probably be feeling these same emotional pains. Knowing they can relate to someone you previously worked with will help them feel like you are the right person for them, too.

Next, focus on what stood out to them about your product or service versus your competition and what was the selling point that made them reach out, connect, and book or buy? Something spoke to them and you want to find out what that was.

And lastly, *hone in on how they have benefited from working with you or purchasing your product.* Remember to dig deeper than the surface. I provide websites for my clients and customers, but I'm also providing a greater sense of confidence in their business, not to mention the ability to maintain their website on their own and not feel lost. They feel like they can continue to grow their website with their business.

How are you improving their life? Figure that out, display it on your website, and connect with more clients just like them.

To send these questions to your client, I recommend automating it a bit. Create a form or a canned email that you can easily send when the time is right! I have a questionnaire form that I send to clients after our project has wrapped up. I ask these three questions as well as a couple other more specific ones and wrap up with a form field where they can provide a summary or testimonial. This allows them to work through the questions I've specifically asked but also gives them an opportunity at the end to piece it all together into a full testimonial that most likely touches on the points intended!

You have something awesome to share with the world. Getting high quality client testimonials and feedback about what you are doing right (or wrong) is only going to help you reach more of your target market and lead to growing your business in an impactful way!

DESIREE DEAN DESIGNS

DESIREEDEANDESIGNS.COM

It can be difficult to differentiate yourself from others in the same creative field. Perhaps you could choose an interesting name or non-traditional branding — or both, like floral designer Desiree Dean Designs. "We wanted to inspire our viewers and allow their creativity to be inspired." Desiree and her designer, Kyla Studios, created a more monochromatic site so visitors will be able to focus on her work. "I always looked at art as a hobby until flowers came along. It was like for the first time in my life, everything made sense." With the hand-drawn bouquets, feminine font pairings, and simple brand photos of Desiree, any visitor will be inspired to contact this floral designer for all their future events.

DESIGNED BY

KYLA STUDIO

KYLASTUDIO.COM

TYPEFACES

Reman Script

QuincyCF Light

Lato Light

AUTHENTIC, CREATIVE FLORAL STYLING

SERVING NJ, NY, & PA

bringing your vision to life

VIEW PORTFOLIO

AUTHENTIC, CREATIVE FLORAL STYLING

SERVING NJ, NY, & PA

bringing your vision to life

VIEW PORTFOLIO

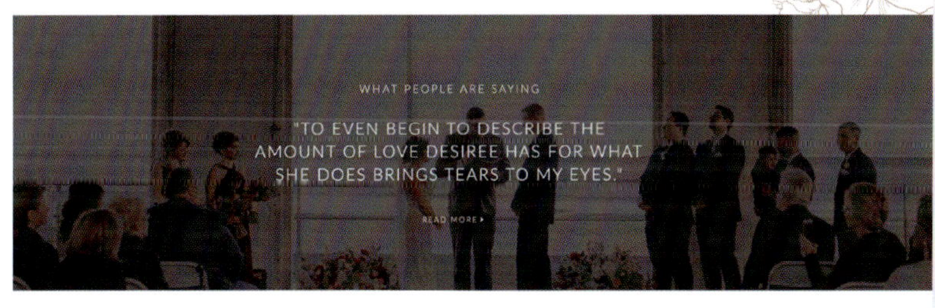

meet desiree

A lover of all things flowers and beauty, in late 2014 Desiree started Desiree Dean Designs. She believed she could create art and flowers allow her the outlet to make that true today. Constantly educating herself and growing within her skill set like the flowers she trusts in, Desiree likes to specialize in weddings and events but never misses an opportunity to connect with someone and to create beauty for special moments in their life. Desiree takes on a select number of events each season to ensure a close relationship with her clients and a balanced family life.

LEARN MORE

FOLLOW US ON INSTAGRAM

HOME

WHAT THEY'RE SAYING

BOTTLEBRUSH FILMS

BOTTLEBRUSHFILMS.COM.AU

Andrew is the cinematographer and Grace is the film editor behind Bottlebrush Films. Together they tell unique wedding stories. Their brand and web design, a nod to film noir, is abstract to appeal to like-minded people looking for more than just a wedding film. "We endeavor to capture our client in all the weird and wonderful ways that make them, them." Working with the designers at Leelou, they collaborated to create an online storefront that's a little post-apocalypse, a little 80s, and has a little bit of a menacing feel. Since the start of their business, Andrew and Grace have found a style that is unapologetically their own, and now they finally have a corner of the web to match.

DESIGNED BY

LEELOU

BYLEELOU.COM

COLORS

#037B85

#CA6036

#211F20

#DBC7AB

#FFFFFF

#C83E33

#F5F5F5

TYPEFACES

ECHOMOTORS

Bebas Bold

Bebas Bold Italic

BEBAS BOOK

BOTTLEBRUSH FILMS

IN A WORLD GONE MAD, LOVE PREVAILED

THESE ARE THOSE STORIES.

STARRING ALICE + JACK

KUITPO | SOUTH AUSTRALIA

STARRING JACK + JULES

STARRING KATE + GABY

ELOPEMENT | OTWAYS

STARRING JAC + LIAM

A LITTLE PARTY NEVER KILLED NOBODY

MELBOURNE | AUS

BOTTLEBRUSH FILMS

IN A WORLD GONE MAD, LOVE PREVAILED

THESE ARE THOSE STORIES...

STARRING ALICE + JACK

LUKE & ASHLEY PHOTOGRAPHY

LUKEANDASHLEY.COM

Fun and relatable are words that you would use to describe Luke and Ashley, as a couple and as a brand. This husband and wife team love to create experiences for their couples to make them feel at ease, and completely catered to — starting with their website. Amongst joyful couples, powerful testimonials, and sweet ways to get to know the photographers, LukeandAshley.com leaves quite the lasting impression on their web visitors. Working with Mark Brand Boutique for the last 3 years, the latest redesign was a breeze. "After we refreshed our site with Mark Brand and Showit, attracting our Ideal Client has been so easy! Our website design was created to ONLY reach our ideal client, and it is paying off!"

DESIGNED BY

ELISE KLUGE
MARK BRAND BOUTIQUE

MARKBRANDBOUTIQUE.COM

COLORS

#191926
#28293E
#61938C
#BC5A93
#FCBB94
#E3D7D7
#EAEAEA
#FFFFFF

TYPEFACES

Playfair Display

Playfair Display Italic

Raleway

Raleway Semi Bold

LUKE & ASHLEY
VIRGINIA
WEDDING
PHOTOGRAPHERS

WE CAPTURE BEAUTIFUL, TIMELESS IMAGES THAT SHOWCASE THE WEDDING DAY IN A VERY AUTHENTIC WAY.

As experienced Virginia wedding photographers, we photograph weddings all over Hampton Roads, Greater Virginia, and world wide.

We offer all our brides a complimentary engagement photo session that will showcase your style and the love you have for one another.

OUR BRIDES AND GROOMS ARE FULL OF LIFE, LOVE AND ENERGY! LET'S HAVE FUN ON YOUR WEDDING DAY!

LUKE & ASHLEY PHOTOGRAPHY

HUSBAND & WIFE WEDDING PHOTOGRAPHY TEAM SERVING HAMPTON ROADS & BEYOND

JODEE DEBES PHOTOGRAPHY

JODEEDEBES.COM

Jodee, the photographer behind this incredible site, is just so full of life and joy. And that joy pretty much smacks you in the face as soon as you enter her online home, designed by the incredible creatives at Northfolk. From the bride being thrown into the air, to the vibrantly colorful images that follow, this site is full of tangible energy! Jodee was aiming for an approachable, professional, yet still fun, kind of vibe. And she nailed it. You have to check out her about section that encourages her visitors to 'go on, hover over'. It is such an interactive way to get to know the person behind the incredible photography! Jodee says her website has been selling her personality even before her clients meet her. What a great first impression!

DESIGNED BY

RACHEL THATCHER & SAM CULP
NORTHFOLK

NORTHFOLK.CO

COLORS

#2A2928

#F2F2F4

#EDDED5

#C4A369

#FFFFFF

TYPEFACES

Latin Modern Roman Regular

Latin Modern Roman Italic

Latin Modern Roman Bold

Open Sans Normal

Open Sans Bold

JODEE DEBES | HOME | IMAGES | ABOUT | SHOP | LEARN | CONTACT | BLOG

capturing real moments + wild adventures

JODEE DEBES

PHOTOGRAPHY

To put it simply:

photography makes me happy

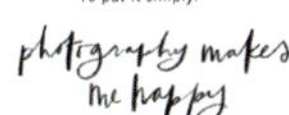

You'll often catch me with a goofy grin on my face as I gallivant around the world capturing memories. My love for photography is equally as great as my love for people, which is why it's a true joy to work with some of the coolest couples, families, and individuals around.

My goal in life is to capture those real moments of laughter, tears and awe, so I love a good candid and always strive to take on a photojournalistic approach with my images. It's thrilling to be invited to document the treasured moments and adventures of remarkable people, and I thank you for allowing me to do what I love.

FUN FACTS

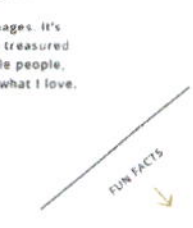

CHANGING THE GAME, ONE PERFECTLY 'GRAMMED PIC AT A TIME

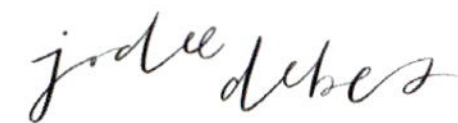

jodee debes

RAVES

"BLUSHING FROM ALL THE SWEET WORDS FROM PAST COUPLES"

Oh - my - god - how on earth could I ever begin to explain how phenomenal Jodee is. Two words - HIRE HER! Not only are her photos absolutely stunning, she is the sweetest and so funny.

STUDIO AAN DE KUST

STUDIOAANDEKUST.NL

Tessa of Studio Aan De Kust (which translates to 'on the coast') was inspired by her everyday life in her seaside town in Holland. The colors, the feeling of the ocean, sand, sunshine, and the breeze all come together on her website. As a graphic designer, Tessa's online storefront was created from a Northfolk design to show off her own design skills, as well as a peak at her studio's offerings. "My website is my first touchpoint with my (potential) customers. This is where I can show my work, who I am, and how I work. Since I've launched this website I've already reached a lot of clients who choose to work with me because of my style." And what great style you have, Tessa!

DESIGNED WITH

BLOCK BY NORTHFOLK

COLORS

#49595C

#658B70

#8DAEB7

#ECEBE8

#FCF0DF

#AB3932

#FBFBFA

TYPEFACES

Quattrocento Bold

Oswald Light

Proxima Nova Semibold

Proxima nova light

Home About Packages  Portfolio Contact Shop

SHOW ME THE GOODS

Packages

Packages

Recent projects

GIMME MORE>

Tessa really has a talent for translating what you cannot express yourself well into a clear concept (without putting the words into your mouth) and then visualizing that. Tessa is approachable, interested and enthusiastic in her approach. An incredibly creative approacher who beautifully visualizes concepts, no matter how vague your concept may be in advance. Highly recommended to professionalize or renew your company!

Suzy Koot | Bureau Lokahi

PHONE
+31 657841783

E-MAIL
INFO@STUDIOAANDEKUST.NL

SOCIAL
@ STUDIO

NAME | E-MAIL | RECEIVE TIPS & TOOLS

AMANDA ADAMS PHOTOGRAPHY

AMANDAADAMS.CO

Amanda Adams is a Maryland wedding and portrait photographer as well as a homeschooling mom of three. Her passion for creating family heirlooms is a driving force for her award-winning photography studio that she built from the ground up after leaving the corporate world. Her online home began as the *Bondi Beach* template by Davey and Krista, which was the perfect fit for her coastal inspired brand. Her work is classic, elegant and timeless and best suited in print, which resounds with her strong belief in leaving beautiful legacies. A storyteller at heart, Amanda's website is host to emotional stories about her heritage, as well as the stories of all the families and couples she has the honor to serve.

DESIGNED WITH

BONDI BEACH BY DAVEY & KRISTA

COLORS

#040404

#C3A990

#C0B8A9

#A6AFB1

#EDDFCE

#EFEEE9

#EEEFF0

#FFFFFF

TYPEFACES

Cormorant Garamond Normal

Cormorant Garamond Italic

Cormorant Garamond Light

Cormorant Garamond Light Italic

Alora Boston

AMANDA
ADAMS
WEDDINGS & PORTRAITS
SCROLL TO EXPERIENCE MORE

HOME
MEET US
WEDDINGS
PORTRAITS
THE BLOG
CONTACT

maryland coastal weddings
WELCOME! I'M SO GLAD YOU'RE HERE.
Finding a wedding photographer that works well with you and your fiancé, and has a style that compliments yours is such an important decision. Hopefully, our website will help you with that! I want nothing more than to make your experience an enjoyable and unforgettable one! Let's take some time to get to know each other a bit better...
EXPLORE OUR WEBSITE

MEET AMANDA
Our story spans oceans and decades of people coming together to build lives they're proud of. So does yours! And having the honor of being able to add to your legacy and take a small role in telling your story is an honor that I can't even begin to put into words.
MEET AMANDA

CAPTURING HEARTFELT, CLASSIC IMAGERY DESTINED TO BECOME FAMILY heirlooms
MENU
AMANDA
ADAMS
SCROLL TO EXPERIENCE MORE

the latest on the blog
Our blog is a huge resource for our couples! You'll find everything from tips for planning for rain on your wedding day to how to properly clean your ring before your portrait session. And of course you'll see lots and lots of posts celebrating our couple's engagements and weddings! Browse our blog and start planning your dream wedding, today!
VISIT THE BLOG

SIGNATURE weddings

CATHERINE GUIDRY PHOTOGRAPHY

CATHERINEGUIDRY.COM

Catherine Guidry is a New Orleans based wedding photographer, educator, and the host of the "Mistakes Make Magic" podcast. Though she holds a Master's Degree in Architecture, photography is her one true passion. Her background in architecture allows her to create imagery that is timeless, unique, and well designed with purpose and intentionality. As a hybrid photographer, her images are elegant and timeless, just like her custom designed website by Davey and Krista. With a neutral color palette and beautiful handwritten fonts, Catherine's site hosts wedding day stories of her couples, her podcast, and abundant opportunities for photographers to learn from her. The site truly organizes everything in a way that allows the visitor to move smoothly through the site, gathering the information most specific to their needs.

DESIGNED WITH

EAST HAMPTON BY DAVEY & KRISTA

COLORS

#838383

#A7A7A7

#134449

#49887F

#92B4B6

#C2CBC6

#E6D9D1

#FFFFFF

TYPEFACES

Questrial Normal

Sundays

EB Garamond Normal

EB Garamond Italic

HOME ABOUT SERVICES **CATHERINE GUIDRY** PHOTOGRAPHY EDUCATION BLOG CONTACT

PINTEREST FACEBOOK INSTAGRAM *elsewhere*

CATHERINE GUIDRY
PHOTOGRAPHY

Passionate about creating professional, organized experiences and modern, memorable images!

Images are what we turn to in order to remember the places we've been, the things we've experienced and the people we've experienced them with. I enjoy documenting life's greatest moments so that you can relive them over and over again through the medium.

Passionate about creating professional, organized experiences and modern, memorable images!

EXPLORE
WEDDINGS
Photography for the Sophisticated Who Know How to Have Fun

LISTEN TO THE
PODCAST
Inspiring creatives to embrace failure and overcome fear in pursuit their greatest entrepreneurial endeavors.

RESOURCES FOR
PHOTOGRAPHERS
Helping photographers tackle great obstacles to build a lasting and successful business.

meet catherine
NEW ORLEANS LIFESTYLE
PHOTOGRAPHER & EDUCATOR

You may have stumbled upon my work through a friend, recommendation or social media. And now here you're...connecting with my simple, bright and natural aesthetic!

Hi! I'm Catherine (also known as "Cat"), a New Orleans based lifestyle photographer and educator. I am a people-pleaser, passionate about creating meaningful experiences and images for clients who value the same!

LEARN MORE

SIGNATURE
WEDDINGS

Il Mercato

SAMANTHA + HAYDEN
Ritz Carlton

TESS + CHRIS
Felicity

SAMANTHA + PATRICK
NOPSI

JENNIFER LARSEN

JENNIFERLARSENPHOTO.COM

Jennifer Larsen may live in New Jersey, but she's a Southern romantic at heart, creating beautiful images for her couples that are timeless and ooze light-hearted romance. With a custom website designed by Davey and Krista, Jennifer's work elegantly tells the love story of each couple she has the honor of photographing. Dripping with neutral and classic details, this visual representation of her brand helps her to convey her mission to the world: "My brand is very warm and friendly, with a heart for southern hospitality. My brand is focused on creating both a level of comfort and friendship and openness." But all this is presented with a high level of quality in the product she delivers, as well as the full experience of working with her.

DESIGNED BY

DAVEY & KRISTA JONES

DAVEYANDKRISTA.COM

COLORS

#4C4C4C

#55524F

#F8F4F1

#EDDAA2

#E0D7D2

#B8B0AB

#DEE4C2

#FFFFFF

TYPEFACES

Questrial Normal

Adobe Devangari

Adobe Devangari Italic

Adobe Devangari Italic Bold

Adobe Devangari Italic Bold Italic

Jennifer Larsen

HOME MEET JEN WEDDINGS PORTRAITS FOR PHOTOGRAPHERS BLOG CONTACT

RELIVING LIFE & LOVE

THROUGH TIMELESS PHOTOS THAT CAPTURE YOUR STORY.

explore the site

explore WEDDING PHOTOGRAPHY ANNIVERSARY

hey there,

I'M JEN LARSEN

I'M A SOUTHERN-AT-HEART WEDDING & ANNIVERSARY PHOTOGRAPHER BASED IN NEW JERSEY, SERVING COUPLES WORLDWIDE.

I love to travel and explore equally as much as I love sipping iced coffee on the couch in my living room. I'm a proud puppy mama to a little maltipoo with a big personality. I am a firm believer in hugging over handshakes, that a house is not a home without a pineapple (or twenty), and that you can never have too many throw pillows.

more about jen

all the details about the

Wedding Experience

EVERYTHING YOU NEED TO KNOW ABOUT WORKING WITH ME TO CAPTURE YOUR START TO FOREVER! HOW DOES THE PROCESS WORK, WHAT'S MY PHILOSOPHY, WHY DO I DO WHAT I DO? LET'S DIVE IN!

my clients have the

SWEETEST THINGS TO SAY

Booking with Jen was *literally* the best wedding planning decision we made.

Aside from being so sweet and caring, Jen is professional, responsive, and extremely talented. She answered all of our many questions in the most timely manner, worked with our schedules, and treated us like cherished clients. She made us feel so comfortable in front of the camera, which lead to more beautiful pictures than we could have EVER imagined. She captured it all and she did it with joy! We (and our family and friends) will be singing her praises forever!

ALANA & BEN

01
02
03
04

BROWSE SOME OF MY

SIGNATURE WORK

TAKE A PEEK THROUGH A SELECTION OF GALLERIES FEATURING WEDDINGS I'VE PHOTOGRAPHED!

Jennifer Larsen

RELIVING LIFE & LOVE

THROUGH TIMELESS PHOTOS THAT CAPTURE YOUR STORY.

explore the site

explore

WEDDING PHOTOGRAPHY

ANNIVERSARY

LAURA & RACHEL

LAURAANDRACHEL.COM

Laura and Rachel are a mother-daughter photography team based in Charleston. In addition to serving wedding and portrait clients with elegant and timeless photography, they're educators with a passion for helping other photographers grow their businesses and elevate their work. Wanderlust has led them across the country serving their clients, and experiencing as many quiet coffee shops as possible. With a custom website by Davey and Krista, their online home is the epicenter of their business — host to beautiful galleries of weddings and families, as well as the home for their educational resources. With neutral colors and nautical elements, their coastal brand is represented in a timeless and elegant design, that is so warm and inviting to all of their website visitors.

DESIGNED BY

DAVEY & KRISTA JONES

DAVEYANDKRISTA.COM

COLORS

#343434

#C7C5C8

#0B2947

#EAD7C8

#EDEBE6

#F9F6F5

#E8E5E3

#FFFFFF

TYPEFACES

Junicode Regular

Junicode Italic

Open Sans Normal

Raleway Normal

Bickham Regular

LAURA & RACHEL
PHOTOGRAPHERS

HOME MEET LAURA & RACHEL FOR BRIDES LIFESTYLE PROPOSALS EDUCATION BLOG CONTACT

HEY THERE! WE'RE

LAURA & RACHEL

Mother-Daughter Wedding Photographers,
Educators,
Believers, Chick-Fil-A Lovers,
Southern Hearted, & Style Obsessed.

OUR STORY

LAURA & RACHEL

HEY THERE! WE'RE

LAURA & RACHEL

NEWLY ENGAGED?

RIGHT THIS WAY!

Hello! Congratulations on your engagement! We're SO glad you're here! Get comfy, grab a cup of coffee, (or wine) and let us share more about our wedding experience.

the details

ARE YOU A

PHOTOGRAPHER?

If so, you're in the right place! There is nothing we love more than serving people and helping their business grow. Click here for more information and be sure to check out our newest workshop dates!

the details

Our wanderlust hearts have taken us all over the country, capturing love stories, and visiting quaint hometown coffee shops along the way, and even though we've spent most of our lives in a nautical California town, we now call South Carolina home, expanding to the low country of Charleston.

BLOG FAVORITES

CARATS & CAKE FEATURE | SANTA LUCIA PRESERVE WEDDING

RJ & ALLY

SOCIAL POP CO.

SOCIALPOPCO.COM

The eye candy that is Jelisa Varnado's site, is so fun, colorful, and sweet, you may get a cavity! Starting off with a design by Elizabeth McCravy, and customized by Ingrid of Penguin Designing, this website is a real treat! The 50 shades of pink make a statement and all of the other colors in the rainbow are the exclamation point! As a marketing strategist catering to female business owners in the beauty and wellness space, Social Pop gets your attention and draws you in. But it's not all looks with no substance. "My brand now matches it's worth! Prior to my new site, my business had no cohesiveness outside of its Instagram page." It's no wonder companies are hiring Social Pop to market their brands in fun and unique ways.

CUSTOMIZED BY

INGRID URENA
PENGUIN DESIGNING

PENGUINDESIGNING.COM

COLORS

#323333
#F27B8C
#EAC1CB
#D1C8DF
#BAE3C3
#F5EECB
#F9DEE4
#FFFFFF

TYPEFACES

Montserrat Bold
Montserrat Medium
Montserrat Normal
Spinwerad

HOME SERVICES OUR WORK ABOUT CONTACT BLOG WORK WITH US

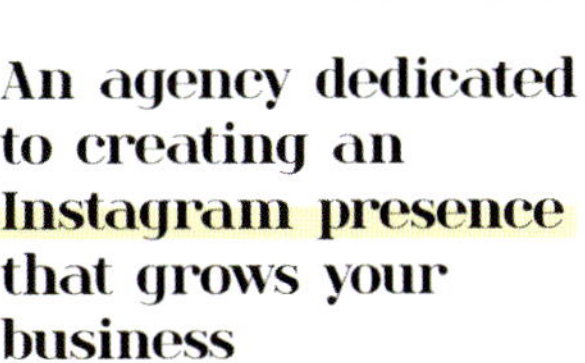

Social Pop Co.

CREATIVE SOCIAL MARKETING

An agency dedicated to creating an Instagram presence that grows your business

IS YOUR INSTAGRAM FEED FULL OF SUB-PAR PHOTOS, GENERIC STOCK IMAGES, AND MESSAGING THAT DOESN'T RESONATE WITH YOUR AUDIENCE?

LET'S FIX THAT

Beauty and wellness are some of the most intimate parts of our lives, so your brand's Instagram needs to be able to build connections rather than sell sell sell. There are a million different options out there when it comes to products and services, so your feed needs to connect to your dream client's hearts, not just their wallets.

If you don't create that connection, you won't see the results you want, and your audience will miss out on the magic of your offer.

YOUR BRAND *IS* A LIFESTYLE

If you have a pair of jeans that are perfect for a unique body type, a foundation for working women, or a stretching sequence that cures a hangover, it's your responsibility to share that with the world.

Those jeans don't just fit perfectly, they empower the women who wear them to feel beautiful. The foundation gives working gals gives the confidence to walk into meetings and burst through every glass ceiling above them. That stretching sequence lets late night partiers do their thing, knowing your remedy will be there for them in the morning.

Without a cohesive visual brand on Instagram that shows the lifestyle you are selling, your brand will remain a hidden little secret.

MENU

Social Pop Co.

CREATIVE SOCIAL MARKETING

An agency dedicated to creating an Instagram presence that grows your business

IS YOUR INSTAGRAM FEED FULL OF SUB-PAR PHOTOS, GENERIC STOCK IMAGES, AND MESSAGING THAT DOESN'T RESONATE WITH YOUR AUDIENCE?

JESSICA LEIGH PHOTOGRAPHY

JESSICALEIGHWEDDINGS.COM

There are so many endearing aspects of Jessica Leigh Weddings that will stand out for brides-to-be. One of the first things you will notice upon entering her site is that she clearly loves outdoor weddings and engagements as those images cascade throughout the site. With the help of Katie from Ribbon & Ink, this house plant enthusiast and lover of natural light wanted to create an online storefront catered to the down-to-earth girl. But paired with the laid back ease, Jessica is very much a Type A personality who strives to serve her amazing brides well. And her first order of business as their photographer is to have her online home a strong, reassuring handshake to welcome visitors into her family of happy clients.

DESIGNED BY

KATIE DURSKI
RIBBON & INK

RIBBONANDINK.COM

COLORS

#898888
#8EA17B
#DAE5DC
#E7E0CD
#F5E5DA
#F6DE7E
#ECEBE8
#FFFFFF

TYPEFACES

Montserrat Light
Palatino
Adore

HOME ABOUT INFORMATION GALLERIES BLOG CONTACT

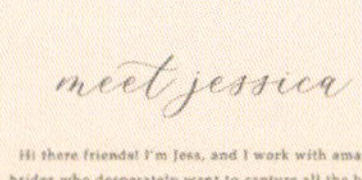

meet jessica

Hi there friends! I'm Jess, and I work with amazing brides who desperately want to capture all the beauty and all the feels on their wedding day while actually enjoying it! I'm a house plant enthusiast, lover of natural light, and green tea addict.

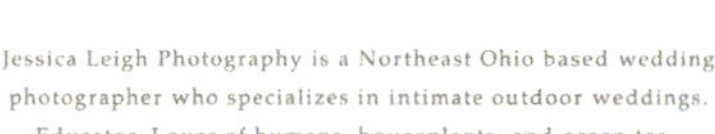

Jessica Leigh Photography is a Northeast Ohio based wedding photographer who specializes in intimate outdoor weddings. Educator. Lover of humans, houseplants, and green tea.

THE JL COUPLES

are best friends

love nature and being outdoors

are fiercely in love

highly value photography for their wedding

care a lot about their tribe

agree that marriage & how you get married is a big deal

are down to earth

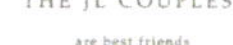

TAKE A LOOK AROUND

browse

VIEW THE

THE JL

GET IN

Welcome

WEDDING PHOTOGRAPHY FOR THE MADLY IN LOVE, ROMANTIC, AND DOWN TO EARTH BRIDES.

Let me tell your story...

CHETTARA T. PHOTOGRAPHY

CHETTARATPHOTOGRAPHY.COM

Is there such a thing as quirky mystical romantic love? There is now, and it can be seen beautifully captured by Chettara of Chettara T. Photography. Desiring to capture magical love stories through a journalistic approach, this website is an adventure in itself. Starting with the *Stella June* design by The Roar, the photographer added a quirky font and her incredible logo, while sticking with the vertical lines that create a subliminal cue to keep scrolling. The minimalist, clean background creates a beautiful canvas that does not compete with her vibrantly moody images. Catering to clients who are "fun, colorful, and madly in love", Chettara's goal is to "weave magical spells through visual tales" for all of her clients.

DESIGNED WITH

STELLA JUNE BY ROAR

COLORS

#0E0E0E

#6F0756

#4B0637

#5E929F

#B87333

#07566F

#F5F5F5

#FDFDFD

TYPEFACES

Siren Song Slant

Farewell Angelina

Chettara T. Photography

NAVIGATE

Genuine

Portrait | Lifestyle |
"I Do" Photography

Philosophy

Photographs are a split second glimpse into life. Freezing a split second in time, so we can look back and remember,

Home
About
Portfolio
Blog
Details
Contact

Genuine

PORTRAIT | LIFESTYLE |
"I DO" PHOTOGRAPHY

Philosophy

Photographs are a split second glimpse into life. Freezing a split second in time, so we can look back and remember, enjoy and/ or reflect. Celebratory times, ordinary times and even sad times... all of your experiences in your life help shape you, define you, enrich you and change you.

I love to photograph those split seconds of your experience, so you can look back and feed your soul with images of where you've gone, who you are and who and what you love to love... and I love to do this by taking pictures of real life... of your real world...not forced smiles, in awkward poses, sitting by a brook. I want you and your every day moments...because let's be real...how much time do you spend posed in a field or forest? I'm betting, not many! Let me capture you and those split seconds of your life, so you can look back and see you, being you...and being with the people and things that you love.

I offer "tale" sessions, telling your own personal narrative.

NORTH PARK FILMS

NORTHPARKFILMS.COM

Is there a better way to tell your story than through videography on your wedding day? Damian Armstrong with North Park Films doesn't think so. And it might appear that he is correct, as his art is displayed as soon as you enter his website. Emotional film of beautiful couples, enjoying the best day of their lives with so much emotion. Much like his work, Damian wanted his website to be timeless. With deep greens and light grays that compliment his personality and work, his minimalist site has been attracting his dream clients who are adventurous and free-spirited. He was inspired by the template *Aspen Willow* designed by Swoone and was able to customize it to fit his brand and vision.

DESIGNED WITH

ASPEN WILLOW BY SWOONE

COLORS

#8C8C8C

#000000

#8C8C8C

#F9F7F6

#FFFFFF

TYPEFACES

Montserrat

Slabo Normal

Shopping Script

NORTH PARK FILMS

LET US TELL YOUR STORY

check out our recent work

OTTAWA WEDDING VIDEOGRAPHER

HOME ABOUT FILMS NORTH PARK FILMS INVESTMENT BLOG CONTACT

LET US TELL YOUR STORY

check out our recent work

OTTAWA WEDDING VIDEOGRAPHER

hello there

Hi! my name is Damian and I am the lead *Ottawa wedding videographer* behind North Park Films.

Everything that matters to me has happened on North Park Street. I met my child hood partner now of 16 years. I discovered my passion for film making and most recently I became a father. North Park is embedded in everything that I am

My goal with North Park Films is to be able to tell your love story giving you a wedding film that is timeless. Simply put I treat every wedding film as if it was my own, I want to give you your own North Park Film telling your love story in a way that is unique, timeless and personal.

I am excited to now serve the *Ottawa, Nepean and Kanata* region. Let us bring your story to life.

EXPLORE THE WEBSITE

your story matters to us

FILMS

INVESTMENT

MEET DAMIAN

WELCOME TO FUTURE

North Park Brides

I know you have a lot of options when it comes to *Ottawa, Nepean or Kanata wedding videographers*, and so I very much appreciate you being here! I truly love & cherish each wedding and all the details & emotions that come along with them. At *North Park Films* Our goal is to deliver a wedding film that is personal, unique and timeless.

The end goal is to give you a film that you can show to your future family that reflects your story and bond. I'm excited to learn more about you!

4+ Years
CREATING TIMELESS WEDDING FILMS

100+ Films
SHOT THROUGHOUT MY CAREER AS A TORONTO & OTTAWA WEDDING VIDEOGRAPHER

3 Team
MEMBERS WHO LOVE TO DOCUMENT LOVE

60+ Couples
WE WERE BLESSED WITH OVER THE AMAZING YEARS

FEATURES

BILZU LIGZDA

BILZULIGZDA.LV

It isn't often you meet a photographer from Latvia, but when you do, it definitely makes one curious to know more. "Beautiful country surrounded by north winds, misty forests and the melancholic dunes of the Baltic Sea" are the inspiration behind Bilzu Ligzda which literally means "a nest of pictures". Whether it's unique weddings, emotional portraits, or spectacular landscapes, intimate and bold images are nestled everywhere on her website that she designed using a Three Fifteen Design template. The color palette is warm and the vibe is vibrant. Linda wants to make sure you get to see the beauty of her country, if not first-hand, at least through her inviting and organic website.

DESIGNED WITH

MAPLE BY THREE FIFTEEN DESIGN

COLORS

- #CBAF8E
- #656F59
- #B7C1AA
- #F6D0B8
- #EAE4DC
- #F2F1EE
- #8E3D19

TYPEFACES

Arapey Italic

Playfair Display Normal

Playfair Display Italic

Playfair Display Heavy

Home
About
Portfolio
Stories
Details
Contact
let's build a nest of memories together
Journal Entries
01.
Portfolio
Let's get closer
02.
About
Price list & information
03.
Details
"Linda is an artist. Everything is noticed at the right time and place, but the same time almost imperceptible."
home
about
portfolio
details
contact
stories
Based in Latvia/ Available for worldwide
© 2020 Bilžu Ligzda
01.
Portfolio
Journal Entries
02.
About
Let's get closer

ELANALOO

ELANALOO.COM

It's like a light breeze hits you when you first pop onto Elana's gorgeous site, elanaloo.com, which she runs with her partner Aaron. Hoping to achieve this merge of nature and technology, they looked to Tonic Site Shop for their custom website design, starting with the *Cosmopolitan* design. Their inspiration came from the ocean, as they are photographers, marketing strategists, and environmental advocates in Hawaii and Maine. Since launching their site, they've been making waves with a site that finally "demonstrates the quality and excellence we provide as a business," empowering more people to also create positive environmental changes in their life while being inspired to live more consciously and intentionally. This site is minimalism, sustainability, and the beauty of technology at its finest.

DESIGNED WITH

COSMOPOLITAN BY TONIC SITE SHOP

COLORS

- #A78F7E
- #D09F7C
- #D5BBA9
- #A3C5BD
- #B67548
- #ECE9E0
- #293845
- #FFFFFF

TYPEFACES

Nunito Sans Bold

Nunito Sans Normal

Maleah Bold

Maleah Regular

MAKING WAVES IN LIFE & BUSINESS
I'm Elana Jadallah
BASED ON THE BIG ISLAND OF HAWAI'I & IN MAINE
I'm a photographer, educator, marketing strategist and environmental advocate that views life & business through the lens of sustainability. Consider me a person with a vision, here to help you clarify and achieve yours!
LET'S GET AQUAINTED

MAKING WAVES IN LIFE & BUSINESS

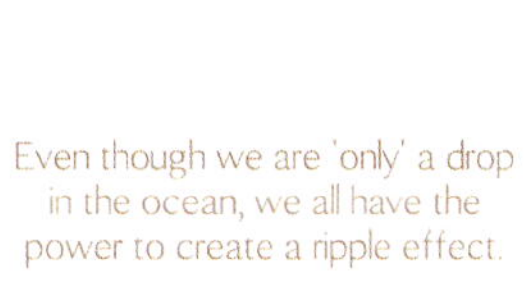
Even though we are 'only' a drop in the ocean, we all have the power to create a ripple effect.
Whether you're an individual looking to deepen your awareness or a creative entrepreneur looking to sustainably grow your business, there's more to discover here. *Select an option below to see how we can make waves.*
i'm looking to:
CHOOSE AN OPTION

MEET
ELANA &
AARON
Formerly, Dérive Collective,
we're a passionate creative duo
LEARN MORE

HOPE TAYLOR

HOPETAYLOR.COM

Hope Taylor's site, designed by Jen Olmstead of Tonic, is swoon-worthy Southern charm at its best. This South Carolina gal is sure to win over anyone who visits the site, be it brides, seniors, or fellow photographers. You will want to stay engaged until every fun detail has been discovered. There are so many unique moving parts, including a Hope fashion show, where you get to see all the many "hats" she wears. "High end, preppy brands that fed inspiration into my website were brands like Kendra Scott, Draper James and Kate Spade. I also pulled inspiration from my home decor, favorite florals and quirky pieces of my personality to help viewers feel like they know me!"

DESIGNED BY

JEN OLMSTEAD

TONICSITESHOP.COM

COLORS & CUSTOM TYPOGRAPHY

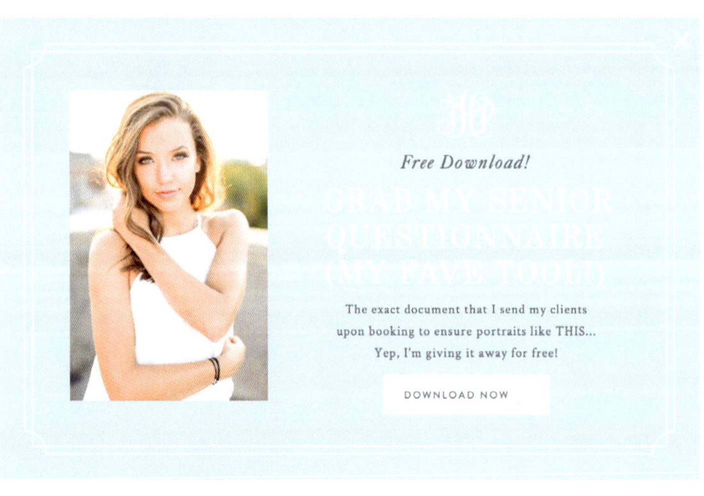

CUSTOM CALLIGRAPHY LOGO

ALL-CAPS WITH EXTRA KERNING

TIMELESS SERIF

CONTRASTING CALL TO ACTION

HOME MEET HOPE WEDDINGS SENIORS EDUCATION CONTACT BLOG NEWSLETTER

HOPE TAYLOR

Hey, Gorgeous!

I'M HOPE TAYLOR

A Charleston photographer for the classic Southern bride, an educator for the hustling photographer and, if we ever go out to dinner, I'll probably order chicken fingers alongside my vodka soda.

I'M SO GLAD YOU'RE HERE!

HOPE TAYLOR

EST. 2013

Hey, Gorgeous!

I'M HOPE TAYLOR

Select Your

EXPERIENCE

I'M A

BRIDE

I'M A

PHOTOGRAPHER

I'M A

SENIOR

GRAB SOME OF MY MOST-POPULAR EDUCATIONAL RESOURCES

HAPPY HOUR WITH HOPE

FREE EDUCATIONAL VIDEOS EVERY WEEK... TUNING IN WITH YOUR FAVE GLASS OF WINE IS ENCOURAGED.

EDUCATION ON THE BLOG

YEARS WORTH OF FREE EDUCATION INCLUDING FREE DOWNLOADS, VIDEOS AND MORE!

FREE DOWNLOAD: MY SENIOR QUESTIONNAIRE

THE EXACT DOCUMENT THAT I SEND MY CLIENTS UPON BOOKING... I'M GIVING IT AWAY FOR FREE!

MEET HOPE

I'm a Southern girl at heart with a deep spiritual connection to buttered popcorn and Christmas-scented candles. Here's all the important stuff you'll need to know to see if we're soul sisters:

Charleston, SC

Strawberry refresher - no berries!

JENNIFER RYALS PHOTOGRAPHY

JENNIFERRYALS.COM

There are happy people, and then there are abundantly out-of-control joyous people. And Jennifer Ryals most definitely falls into the latter category. That joy overflows even onto her website. As soon as you enter her space, you are greeted with giant smiles and glorious laugh lines. She wanted a website where her clients could visualize themselves in the images, and they are doing just that! "I get compliments ALL the time from my clients and other vendors, and it has definitely helped my conversion rate to increase because Showit is just so much easier for clients to navigate." Whether it's the vibe of her website, the stunning *Rosé Royale* Tonic template that she customized, or a glorious marriage of both, jenniferryals.com is a happy online home to visit anytime you need a pick me up...or a wedding photographer!

DESIGNED WITH

ROSÉ ROYALE BY TONIC SITE SHOP

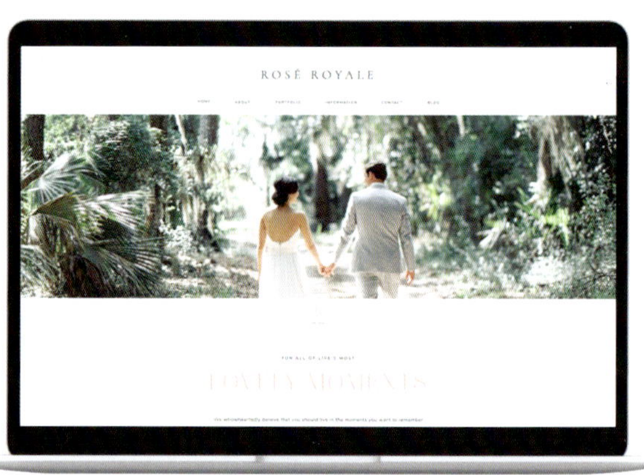

COLORS

#E3BFB6

#19191A

#575757

#F4E6E1

#285A15

#FBF9F9

#ECEBE8

#FFFFFF

TYPEFACES

Aire Bold Pro

CARRIG REFINED ROMAN

Nunito Sans Normal

EB Garamond Italic

JENNIFER RYALS

Love Hard MY STORY INVESTMENT THE IMAGES BLOG CONTACT *Serve Well*

IF YOU'RE LOOKING FOR A PHOTOGRAPHER THAT FEELS LIKE A LONG LOST FRIEND,

And if you just want a photographer, hire her because there is no one better.

Loren E.
Jennifer Ryals Photography Bride

info@jenniferryals.com

HI, I'M JENNIFER!

TIMELESS AND JOYFUL IMAGES WITHOUT THE AWKWARD.

Stories are how we connect as humans and photos are what we use to tell those stories for generations to come and I can't wait to hear yours. You are celebrating your biggest moment with the people that matter most, and I want to help you capture that in a way that's genuine and thoughtful. Your wedding is going to be one of the best chapters in your incredible story, and you deserve to flip through those pages 30 years from now with absolutely no regrets. I am here to get you there.

Learn more about MY story, right here...

01 ABOUT JENNIFER

02 VIEW MY WORK

03 INVESTMENT

04 INQUIRE

JENNIFER RYALS

NAVIGATE

Love Hard

EST. 2016

Serve Well

IF YOU'RE LOOKING FOR A PHOTOGRAPHER THAT FEELS LIKE A LONG LOST FRIEND,

hire Jennifer.

And if you just want a photographer, hire her because there is no one better.

- Loren E.
Jennifer Ryals Photography Bride

SAN ANTONIO, TEXAS + WORLDWIDE

JENNIFER CLAPP PHOTOGRAPHY

JENNIFERCLAPPPHOTOGRAPHY.COM

Jennifer is a fine art film photographer who is passionate about capturing people's love stories. Her site, JenniferClappPhotography.com, highlights nostalgic and romantic weddings and creates an air of delicate romance. She captures and creates timeless images that will never go out of style. Working with designers from With Grace and Gold, they built a site from scratch so that Jennifer would be able to display her images to capture her ideal clients' attention. And since the launch of her new site, she has been able to do just that. And lucky for us, even though California is home, Jennifer travels the world with her camera, eagerly capturing love stories for weddings, engagements, and lifestyle events.

DESIGNED BY

KELLY ZUGAY & ANDRA BARKEY
WITH GRACE & GOLD

WITHGRACEANDGOLD.COM

COLORS

#5D574C
#635E67
#E7E3DF
#E8E8E7
#C0BCC3
#E1CDBE
#F4ECE8
#FFFFFF

TYPEFACES

Melika
ENGRAVERS
Derivia
Brandon Grotesque
Tenor Sans Normal
Martel Normal

MENU

HOME

ABOUT

EXPERIENCE

CONTACT

JOURNAL

JENNIFER CLAPP

FINE ART PHOTOGRAPHY

SERVING CALIFORNIA AND DESTINATION

01 02 03 04

PREV / NEXT

FINE ART FILM PHOTOGRAPHY

FOR THE TIMELESS AND NOSTALGIC IN LOVE

PHOTOGRAPHER · FRIEND

At Jennifer Clapp Photography, I serve couples that appreciate the nostalgic, romantic, dreamy and timeless look of film photography. My photography has taken me around the world, but I love shooting in my home state of California.

At JCP, I create an unforgettable experience for my clients – from the moment we meet in consultation, to your wedding day. I am *all* about getting to know couples, their love stories, what they love about each other, *the* Proposal, their families, and just how it all began. Because, well, *I am a sucker for a good love story.*

LEARN MORE →

THE WEDDING EXPERIENCE

LEARN MORE →

"SHE IS EXTREMELY TALENTED, AND IT SHOWS IN THE QUALITY OF HER WORK."

– BROOKE AND DAVID

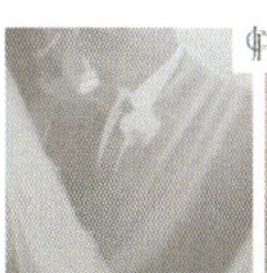

@JENCLAPPPHOTO

JENCLAPPSTUDIO@GMAIL.COM

JENNIFER CLAPP

FINE ART PHOTOGRAPHY

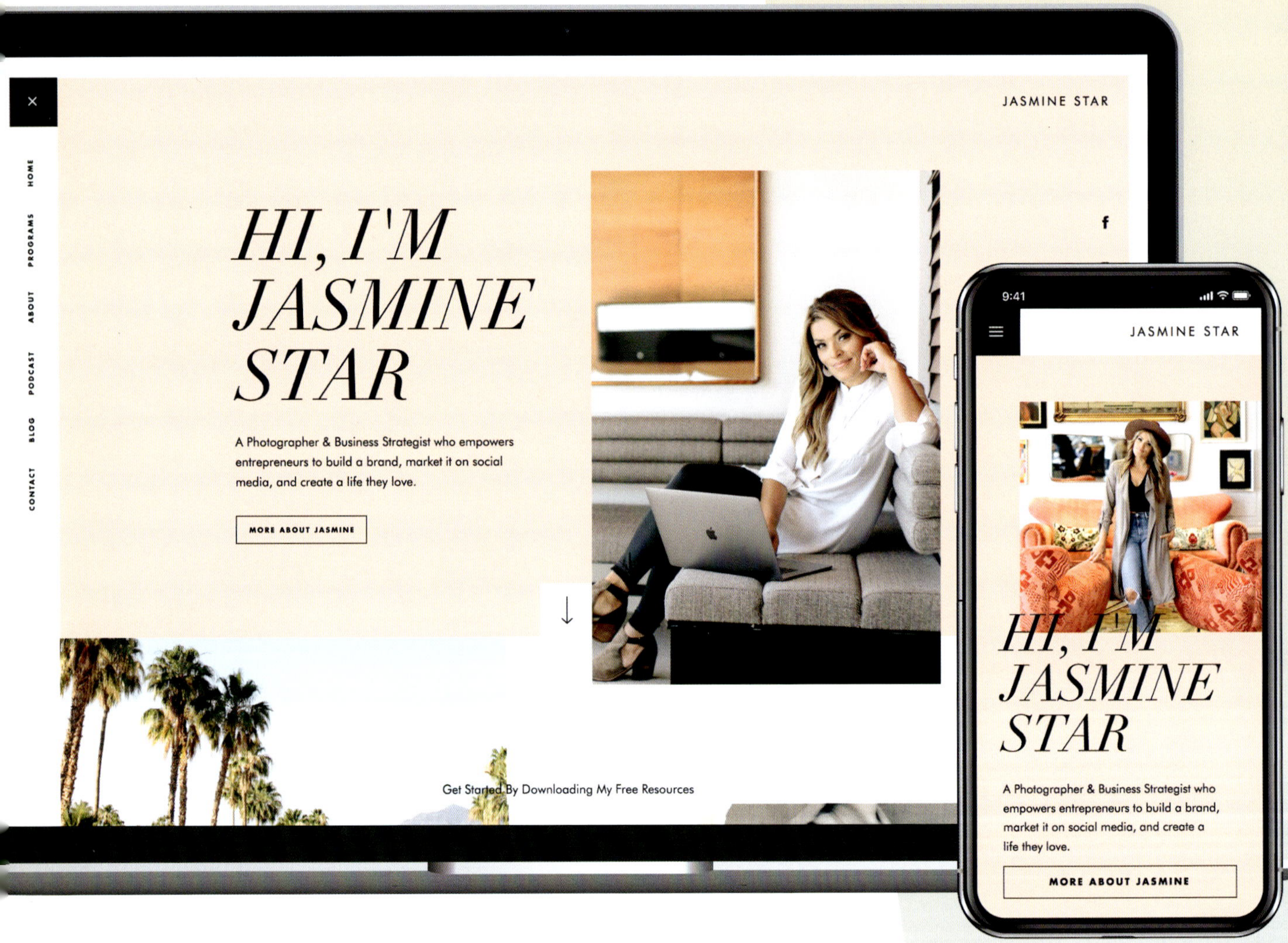